Sarah's Daughters Sing

The Editing Committee

Michelle Bender
Enid Dame
Marion D. S. Dreyfus
Florence B. Freedman
Marian Goldhamer
Annette Bialik Harchik
Cecile Low
Helen Papell
Adena Potok
Mindy Rinkewich
Lucy Cohen Schmeidler

Sarah's Daughters Sing

A Sampler of Poems by Jewish Women

Prepared by the Poetry Project
of the Jewish Women's Resource Center
A project of National Council of Jewish Women
New York Section

Edited by HENNY WENKART

KTAV Publishing House, Inc.
HOBOKEN, N.J.

Library of Congress Cataloging-in-Publication Data

Sarah's daughters sing : a sampler of poems by Jewish women/prepared by the Poetry Project of the Jewish Women's Resource Center, a project of National Council of Jewish Women, New York Section : edited by Henny Wenkart.
    p. cm.
    ISBN 0-88125-348-0.   —ISBN 0-88125-349-9 (pbk.)
    1. Jewish poetry—Women authors. I. Wenkart, Henny. II. Jewish Women's Resource Center. Poetry Project.
PN6109.5.S27   1990
808.81'0082—dc20   89-28686
                                                                                      CIP

Manufactured in the United States of America

Copyright © 1990 by the Jewish Women's Resource Center

The Jewish Women's Resource Center is a project of
National Council of Jewish Women, New York Section
Nancy Rubinger, President

The Artists

	On pages
Brynna Bloomfield	111
Laurie Drehmel	121, 189, 242
Karen Kahn-Stamatis	53, 60, 123, 130, 132, 152, 217, 233, 236, 237, 241, 246, 247
Ruth Paradise	147, 156
Renata Stein	9, 11, 210
Miriam Stern	16, 25, 29, 34, 67, 94, 163, 164, 166, 167, 168, 170, 172, 183, 218, 219
Bracha Turner	93, 116, 117, 196, 204, 223
Tsirl Waletzky	1, 39, 73, 77, 79, 80, 83, 87, 109, 137, 191, 229, 250

The Poems

I. CHAYE SARAH   1

1. Eve   2
   Else Lasker-Schüler

2. Eden   2
   Jacqueline Lapidus

3. Original Sin: A Causal Analysis   4
   Louise Jaffe

4. Her Earrings   6
   Mindy Rinkewich

5. Mitzvah   7
   Maggie Mohr

6. Hagar, The Second Morning: A Midrash   8
   Helen Papell

7. Sarah: Cheshbon Hanefesh   10
   Mindy Rinkewich

8. Sarah Talks to God   12
   Lillian Elkin

9. Confession to Mother Sarah   13
   Annette Bialik Harchik

10. Sarah and Isaac Her Son: A Midrash   13
    Helen Papell

11. A Midrash on Leah   14
    Lynn Saul

12. Leah   15
    Barbara D. Holender

13. Leah Tells Rachel She Wants To Learn Not To Let Jacob Matter . . .   16
    Lynn Saul

14. Rachel's Hunger   17
    Helen Papell

15. Rachel   18
    Barbara D. Holender

16. Sisters   18
    Rosa Felsenburg Kaplan

17. Princess Michal's Song   22
    Rosalind Darrow

18. Michal   23
    Rachel Blaustein

II. AMOL IZ GEVEN

25

1. Brushing   26
   Madeline Tiger

2. Names   29
   Ruth Daigon

3. Braids   30
   Layle Silbert

4. Gey Klap Dem Kop in Vant   30
   Mildred Brenner Pollner

5. Saul's Hammer   31
   Dina Elenbogen

6. Maggid   32
   Marge Piercy

7. Farewell Earth   33
   Peninnah Braude

8. Rozhinkes Mit Mandlen   34
   Irene Javors

9. My Next Door Neighbour   38
   Mindy Rinkewich

10. Boiled Wine   40
    Lucy Cohen Schmeidler

11. They Did Not Build Wings for Them   41
    Irena Klepfisz

12. Rosie   43
    Nicole Lieberman

13. The Beggar in the Subway   44
    Helen Papell

14. Subway Song   45
    Lucy Cohen Schmeidler

15. Poetry   46
    Annette Bialik Harchik

16. Jabotinsky Street   47
    Dina Elenbogen

17. Growing Up   49
    Dina Elenbogen

18. Sister Prophecy: A Gift for Bonita's 32nd Birthday   51
    Celia Y. Weisman

III. THAT YOUR LIFE MAY BE LONG   53

1. Song For My Father   54
   S. Ben-Tov

2. Fathers   55
   Cecile L. Martindale

3. The Rock   55
   Natalie R. Sheffler

4. Momma Remembers   56
   Elaine Mitchell

5. The Depression   59
   Dina Elenbogen

6. Learning Bones   62
   Rhina P. Espaillat

7. Six O'Clock News   63
   Ruth Daigon

8. 1932   64
   Lynn Saul

9. 1940   65
   Madeline Tiger

10. Belonging   66
    Layle Silbert

11. Cactus   68
    Irena Klepfisz

12. Not Yet Visible   69
    Ruth Daigon

13. The Seasons of the Swastika   70
    Henny Wenkart

14. Safe House   72
    Henny Wenkart

15. Coming Home   74
    Eva Reisman

16. Neighborhoods   76
    Enid Dame

17. My Mother's Novel   84
    Marge Piercy

18. On Borrowed Time   85
    Elizabeth Zelvin

IV. LOVE   87

1. Young Women Leave Home   88
   Rifka Fingerhut

2. California Sister . . . 88
   Elizabeth Zelvin

3. Rites de Passage . . . 90
   Madeline Tiger

4. My Father's Garden . . . 91
   Dina Elenbogen

5. April . . . 94
   Henny Wenkart

6. Desire . . . 95
   S. Ben-Tov

7. Patience . . . 97
   Jessica Lipsky

8. Effort at Speech Between Two People . . . 97
   Muriel Rukeyser

9. Predestination or, Love is Not enough . . . 99
   Florence B. Freedman

10. zip-door johnny . . . 99
    Marion D. S. Dreyfus

11. Secrets of the Therapeutic Relationship . . . 101
    Elizabeth Zelvin

12. The Yosom . . . 102
    Blu Greenberg

13. Antonio's Night . . . 104
    Lynn Saul

14. old softie . . . 105
    Marion D. S. Dreyfus

15. A Confession . . . 106
    Judith Heineman

16. In Lieu of Letters . . . 107
    Sharon Cameron

17. Living in Sin . . . 108
    Adrienne Rich

18. Words for a Song 109
    Helen Neville

V. HAREY AT 111

1. Mazel Tov! 112
   Merle Feld

2. Cutting the Jewish Bride's Hair 112
   Ruth Whitman

3. Why I Understand World Literature 113
   Shulamith Surnamer

4. Meditation on Aleph 116
   Lucy Cohen Schmeidler

5. Bedecken 117
   Henny Wenkart

6. Elegy 118
   Madeline Tiger

7. Once More With You 119
   Helen Papell

8. The First Time We Made Shabbos Together 120
   Merle Feld

9. You Sowed in Me, Not a Child 121
   Celia Dropkin

10. Housewife 122
    Susan Fromberg Schaeffer

11. Continuing 124
    Madeline Tiger

12. The Enemy is the Dark 125
    Phyllis Koestenbaum

13. Sunday 125
    Marcia G. Rosen

14. A Woman of Valor, Who Can Find? 126
    Renee Alfandary

15. Housing Shortage *Naomi Replansky*	128
16. The Contract *Sherry Reiter*	129
17. My Jewish Life Line *Peninnah Schram*	131
18. Widow *Florence B. Freedman*	132

VI. DI KINDER — 137

1. Her Eyes Tell Me *Helen Papell*	138
2. Shopping Advice *Henny Wenkart*	138
3. A Mother's Tisha B'Av, July 1984 *Annette Bialik Harchik*	140
4. Prayer on the Approach of Accouchement *Fanny Neuda*	140
5. So Open We Conceive *Chana Bell*	141
6. The Field Anthropologist Gives Birth *S. Ben–Tov*	143
7. My Friends Baked Cake and We Ordered Lox and Whitefish from the Deli *Merle Feld*	145
8. Babies *Madeline Tiger*	145
9. Heartbeat *Henny Wenkart*	148
10. Croup *Merle Feld*	150

11.	Prayers For a Sick Daughter *Madeline Tiger*	151
12.	Nine *Elizabeth Zelvin*	154
13.	Bar Talking *Gayle Spanier Rawlings*	155
14.	Dayeni *Shulamith Surnamer*	156
15.	tah shema *Shulamith Surnamer*	157
16.	Photo-Finish Brat *Marion D. S. Dreyius*	159
17.	Nancy's Aliyah *Cyrille Kane*	160
18.	Partings *Florence B. Freedman*	161

VII. EYT ZIKNAH   163

1.	Old People at the Film Series at the Museum of Modern Art *Ruth Daigon*	164
2.	Louder, Please *Florence B. Freedman*	165
3.	My Mother-in-Law's Name is Rose *Helen Papell*	166
4.	Anna, My Mother-in-Law *Merilee Kaufman*	167
5.	Companions *Michelle Bender*	168
6.	Erasures *Ruth Daigon*	169
7.	Sclerotic *Enid Dame*	171

8. Gray Hairs 172
   Naomi Replansky

9. Therapist 172
   Ruth Roston

10. The Hardest Work of All 173
    Madeline Tiger

11. Houseguest 174
    Michelle Bender

12. Newark 175
    Madeline Tiger

13. The Kohain's Wife 176
    Shulamith Surnamer

14. Round 177
    Layle Silbert

15. A Lifetime's Yizkor 178
    Miriam Bat Or

16. I never think of myself as waiting for you 179
    Merle Feld

17. Elegy for My Father 180
    Henny Wenkart

18. Kri'ah 180
    Henny Wenkart

VIII. ANI MA'AMIN 183

1. If 184
   Rose Gutman-Jasny

2. I cannot swim 184
   Irena Klepfisz

3. Abutilon in Bloom 187
   Irena Klepfisz

4. Childhood Memory 188
   Irene Grimberg

5. Hallo, Hallo   188
   Cecile Low

6. I Dreamed Him Homeward   190
   Yala Korwin

7. Warsaw Carousel   191
   Cecile Low

8. First Thoughts: On Liberation Day From a Concentration Camp   192
   Annette Bialik Harchik

9. Earrings   193
   Annette Bialik Harchik

10. Kol Nidre   194
    Rosa Felsenburg Kaplan

11. Twilight Zone   196
    Mindy Rinkewich

12. Four Jewish Syrian Daughters   197
    Ada Aharoni

13. Kiddush Levana   198
    Ruth Finer Mintz

14. Thinking About the Future of Jerusalem   199
    Shirley Kaufman

15. The Letter I Wanted to Write, The Letter I Wrote, for Osnat, an Ethiopian Student in Israel   200
    Dina Elenbogen

16. Beta Israel   202
    Annette Bialik Harchik

17. Passover 1988   202
    Helen Papell

18. The Last Person Out of the Country, Please Turn Off the Lights   203
    Dina Elenbogen

IX. NACHAMU   205

1. Seasons of Torah   206
   Nancy Lee Gossels
   Joan Kaye
   Rosie Rosenzweig

2. I Know Not Your Way   208
   Malka Heifetz Tussman

3. Sabbath Eyes   208
   Nancy Lee Gossels

4. The Maabaroth   212
   Rikudah Potash

5. In This Galaxy Flowing with Milk and Honey   213
   Shulamith Surnamer

6. Sabbath   215
   Helen Papell

7. Paean After Snow   216
   Louise Jaffe

8. Birdsong & Sun Poem for Winter   218
   Madeline Tiger

9. Tu B' Shevat   219
   Annette Bialik Harchik

10. The Sun and I   220
    Rachel Fishman

11. Sunflowers   220
    Dina Elenbogen

12. Bible Students In The Sukkah   222
    Barbara D. Holender

13. The Crossing   223
    Patricia Moger Varshavtchik

14. We All Stood Together   224
    Merle Feld

15. Yiddish   225
    Layle Silbert

16. The Influence Coming into Play: The Seven of Pentacles   226
    Marge Piercy

17. Haj   227
    S. Ben-Tov

18. Qiryat Shmoneh   228
    Esther Cohen

X. SARAH'S DAUGHTERS   229

1. Holy Grandmothers in Jerusalem   230
   Esther Raab

2. A Letter to the Sons of Abraham   231
   Marica Falk

3. The Girls That are Wanted   232
   Marie Odlum

4. Minor Surgery   233
   Marion D. S. Dreyfus

5. God Only Knows   234
   Malka Heifetz Tussman

6. The Act of Bread   235
   Ruth Whitman

7. I Know About the Woman Who Sits and Waits   236
   Judith Rose

8. Parve   238
   Nina Judith Katz

9. Risa   239
   Marcia Falk

10. light river   240
    Marion D. S. Dreyfus

11. We Are   242
    Elaine Starkman

12. I Am Proud of You   243
    Chana Safran

13. Ancestor   244
    Frances Rodman

14. The Limitations of Therapy   245
    Elizabeth Zelvin

15. Susan Dances   246
    Beth Joselow

16. B'Not Sarah   247
    Shulamith Surnamer

17. Small Pleasures   248
    Nancy Imberman Tamler

18. Women's Talk   249
    Helen Papell

Glossary   251

Index of First Lines   259

Index of Last Lines   262

IN MEMORIAM

Marie Stein Goldstern and Rose Stein Wenkart

DEDICATION

On a June evening in the mid-eighties of the twentieth century Jewish women poets were called together at Council House on Sixty-ninth Street off Central Park. For the first time we read to an audience that never asked us why our poems were female or what made them Jewish. The relief, the lightness of that evening matched the gentle June air and light outside the windows.

Our hostess, who had called us together from her home in Los Angeles, could not be with us that first night because of tragedy in her family. But Marcia Cohn Spiegel, "Marty", has been very much with us since then, physically and through her example and inspiration.

Marty had prepared an immense anthology of poems by Jewish women through the ages that had not yet found a publisher. Some of those poems have appeared in another sampler on the West Coast, and one quarter of the present volume is selected from her original group of poems.

Following our second poetry reading we formed our workshop, which meets winter and summer on the first Tuesday of the month — a sister workshop to the one founded by Marty on the West Coast. Some of the poets in this book who live in places between these two workshops are expanding the Jewish women's poetry network now by organizing new workshops and readings.

To our godmother, then, our Kvatterin, Marcia Cohn Spiegel, SARAH'S DAUGHTERS SING is dedicated with our love.

Chaye Sarah

Eve
by Else Lasker-Schüler

Deep over me you bent your head,
With golden hair and black, black eyes,
And your lips were silken-soft, and red
As the blossoming trees in Paradise.

My soul is love, the birth of love,
O, my soul is yearning and banishment;
You tremble with the fears of grief,
Afraid of what your dreams portend.

Heavy upon your life I lie,
From my womb a thousand fruits will spring.
You, young as earth! you adam-young,
You bent your head deep over me —

Early 1900s   Germany and Israel.
Translated from German by Michael Stone

Eden
by Jacqueline Lapidus

ever since I discovered
Lilith, things
have been different around here

the first time we met
by accident   she
came back one night
for a seashell she'd forgotten to pack

Adam was asleep
and I, restless, strolling
in the orchard
climbed the apple tree
for exercise and heard her
singing in its branches

touch me, she said, see
how my flesh fits
the folds and hollows
of your body   smell
the flower between my legs
feel my muscles
listen to the life
in my womb

   oh, she was beautiful!
I thought I had never seen
anyone quite like her
before next morning, though
bathing in the waves
her image came dancing to me
like sunlight, reflecting
myself

now I go looking
for Lilith everywhere
inventing with her names
for swallow   quartz   anemone
learning to breathe like
dolphins, laughing as our bellies grow
round as the moon

Adam
notices but says nothing
this knowledge of our power
sticks in his throat

Original Sin: A Causal Analysis
by Louise Jaffe

I needed a sin
An original sin
Not your older-type
Early-day
Garden-snake sin
Not your me-too
Count-me-in
Copy-cat sin.
I needed my name
My personword name
Not my Mrs. Lot
Me-forgot
Family-plot name.
I wanted to be
Just (s)infamous me
Not some drag-along baggage
Of Biblical he
From those two sizzling cities
Like mock property.
I needed a way
To make the world say,
"How inventive!" (preventive
Of label cliché.)
With fratricide trite
And lust stale delight

I needed my reason
To seek copyright
And let them suspect
I'd a brain in my head
And was more than flesh pillow
For Lot's nuptial bed.
So I dreamed me a sin
An original sin
Not your any-old
Not-too-bold
Cuckolding sin
Not your matricide/patricide
Clean sweep of kin
But a looking-back
Local-track
Different-tack sin.
Then some questioners came
And asked me my name
(My last chance to savor
My sin-flavored fame)
But I couldn't recall
Felt like thickening wall
Heard them whisper, "Her fault
She's turned pillar of salt."
When I needed a voice
And movespace to rejoice
I became mute past tense
Travestied recompense
Fast-frozen in fame
In my husband's name.

Her Earrings
by Mindy Rinkewich

Sarah gave Hagar to Abraham; and when Ishmael was born she became so jealous that she could no longer live with Hagar. On one occasion she swore that she would not rest satisfied until her hands had been dipped in Hagar's blood, whereupon Abraham immediately pierced Hagar's ears so that the blood might be on Sarah's hands. Such was the origin of the wearing of earrings.

— Arab Legend

Daughters of Sarah
Of Hagar
Of everybody
The earrings
The ear rings
    rings that link
    the generations
The prized souvenir of that old cat fight
The kaffeeklatch that never ends

— I wanted them pierced
   It's so simple
   But then my husband said no
   And I want those earrings so badly
— Then why did you ask him, you dope?
— He said, "Don't make holes in your body."
— Well didn't he do that to you?
— Will you shut up
   The children will hear you
   Come on, girls. Just let's keep it clean
— I like silver with blue
   You get contrast
— And also with purple and black
— Red doesn't look bad with it either

But green things should always have gold
— I'd wear copper with green if I had some
  Would copper infect our ears?
— Do you think that Sarah will wear them?
— She's so old it won't help if she does.

And so the discussion continues
And so the chips fall where they fall
Forever and ever and ever
While the Lords of our Universe run things
And we try to get them to look.

Mitzvah
by Maggie Mohr

It is said that Abraham's tent
had four flaps that were always open
so that all in need could freely enter.
She kept a broomstick lodged in her door,
holding it open to neighbors and friends
A sign that whatever was to be shared
was to be shared, her coffee, a simple roll,
an ear deep and quiet as a cave into which
they could stow their hearts and minds.

Sarah baked bread from her finest flour,
and washed the feet of the three strangers.
This tenement wife, dispensing her cakes,
cleansed a different sediment,
walking silently in the paths of her ancestors.

Hagar, the Second Morning: A Midrash
by Helen Papell

Where are we? my Ishmael sings
to the desert hills. Here, they answer,
here.

And You, God? were You the sun
pointing west
after Abraham disappeared somewhere?
At noon it broke into hot sand
filling my throat.

Twilight cooled the sun like a cloud
of pale wine. Was that You? I sang thanks
until it froze into a cloak of frost
my Ishmael shivered under.

This dawn
a wind moaned like a mother
awakening to her dead child.

Sun scrapes my face,
the water flask is empty,
hawks will soon surround
the last breadcrumb.
My Ishmael sings where
to the hills echoing here, here,
and my eyes open knowing
Abraham intends never to return,
remembering he walked with my son
everywhere but here.

9

Sarah: Cheshbon Hanefesh
by Mindy Rinkewich

I know I don't look too good
But could I have looked better?
He puts me through tests beyond my endurance
He puts up walls many times my height for me to scale
He strikes a high, fast note
And orders me to dance to a tune only an acrobat could follow

Does he despise me for lacking the strength he never gave me?
Not that I am entirely without strength
What man has the guts it took
For me to bring Hagar to Abraham?
Then that Godly trick he played on me
Giving me a son after the birth of her son
Whom I had prepared myself to love
If not for my baby. . . .
Oh hell!
If not for my baby
We still would have had that big fight
If not over a child
It would have been over my authority
                      or her privileges
                      or my jealousy
                      or hers
Abraham still would have yelled:
   —You bitches, be quiet, I tell you!
   —Can't a man have a moment of peace?
Had I done this, that or the other
The tunnel was sealed at both ends from the start.

11

Sarah Talks to God
by Lillian Elkin

"And Abraham stretched forth his hand, and took the knife to slay his son."

And why, Oh King, my God, should the blood of a child
Run precious in your house.
My small boy has brought wheat to your altar
and in the summer gathered fruits and wild flowers.
What will you do with small fingers
and the fright of little hands.
More feeble is he than a bird on your altar
and his heart is a wing.
If we have sinned against your greatness
we have been humble too.
And in the shadows of your timeless sandals
the small gods were weeds.
We have set our house for your guests
and I have brought water and blessed their coming.
I have left the home of familiar herds and shepherds
and my mother's loom is silent.
I have wept in strange lands
but never have I questioned Abraham or his will
which was your own.
But I am a woman and this is my child
and my love for him is greater than fear
and my sorrow surrounds me with knives
and I am bitter in my doubts.

First published in Pioneer Woman.

Confession to Mother Sarah
by Annette Bialik Harchik

You were luckier than I
albeit in your old age
you were granted a son,
though he too was
targeted for loss.
Sharp as the knife
Of Isaac's near sacrifice
was the grief that cut you down.
Not beauty nor wealth nor prestige
could you barter
for the bonds of a loving child.
And I, Sarah,
stand on my own Mt. Moriah
about to join you.

Sarah and Isaac Her Son: A Midrash
by Helen Papell

Abraham's eyes blaze the command to bathe his son
in fire. "Not my son," says Sarah, mother.
"I didn't promise my son's breath to the fiery throat
of the bull-god Moloch in the pagan ravine,
Or to the snakes of the goddess that writhe like clouds
on the pagan mountain.
If my child's sweet sorrowing bones shall crumble
in the wind,
Would the grass of the desert grow greener?
Would the spring flow sweeter?"

Sarah carries a jug to sands awaiting rain.
"My husband has taken Isaac on a journey
that might explode upon you the stones of the sun.
I give you a green path,
I ask that you rise and surround Abraham's first day
Until his eyes cool."

Sarah pulls a noose of leaves that had choked
a spring's throat as dry as Hagar
banished long ago
to the desert by Sarah, mother, wife.
"My husband has taken Isaac on a journey
that might explode into you the leaves of all trees.
I give you a door open to the clouds,
I ask that you rise and freeze Abraham's second day
Until his eyes cool."

On the third day, Abraham sees a ram
white as a cloud of sand,
trussed in leaves like Isaac.
His eyes cool, his hand convulses like a snake striking.
Sarah hears the smoke of sacrifice hiss
past the mountain. "What is the name of a woman
whose son has died?" she asks the desert,
Weeping for Hagar's forgiveness as though it were a trail
she might follow.

First published in Response, *1986*

A Midrash on Leah
by Lynn Saul

Nowadays your father couldn't play his trick,
disguise your awkward body with a veil,
send you to your sister's wedding bed,

then give your husband your pretty sister, too.
Your modern husband chose you by himself
during the time you were thin, or because

that year he liked the poems that you wrote,
or because, after a night in a dark bar (the modern veil)
he got you pregnant. But when the novelty wears off

or passion goes the way of dirty dishes,
while you're in the kitchen saucing his favorite *pasta al dente*,
or in the library finishing your dissertation

he'll go back to your slender sister Rachel.
Even today, he'll have her too.

Leah
by Barbara D. Holender

If I squint I can see him in the field, that Jacob,
the shape that isn't a tree or a sheep.

When my sister goes out with her lunch basket
I watch till two shapes melt and sink.

They could do anything to me, those two,
and I wouldn't see it until it was too late.

Laban tells me I have all the power.
You're the one who's bearing sons, he says.

But there they go in the field,
my sister and our husband,

and here I sit in my tent
exercising power.

Leah Tells Rachel She Wants to Learn Not to Let Jacob Matter . . .
by Lynn Saul

Remember the hill where we played
near our father's home? When we were girls
we would take the sheep there
and talk — I talked,
you laughed.

An acacia tree
clung to a wedge
of rock.

We could see the desert
stretch south toward Bethel
like a clean blanket
that might have room
for us both.

Rachel's Hunger
by Helen Papell

I've seen Rachel tear at the strings
that sew her womb closed.
She's my sister, I don't know why
my babies drop like snowflakes.

I held her in my arms and said
Jacob loved her, she didn't need
a baby to bind him.
Her hungry eyes licked at the skin
of every passing child.

I was born a root-healer. Why else
are my legs short and my eyes twisted?
My teacher said the caves we crawl in
are our mothers and give us milk.
But powder of snake
killed on the entrance floor
didn't ease Rachel's hunger cramps
for a child,
and after mandrake tea
she fell into a sleep
waking only to sing lullabies to a doll.

I took Rachel to the cave of crystals
that tie roof to floor
with frozen strings.
She crawled to it on her belly
and suckled
until the shadow of a child's hand
touched her face.

Rachel
by Barbara D. Holender

I will sit here very still
till I am sure
this life in me is not my life
this pulse my pulse.
I will not tell a soul
until I'm sure.

When big-bellied Leah calls me a dry well
I'll weep as usual and take to my tent.
Jacob runs from family squabbles;
he'll keep his distance for a while.

But when he says, "Enough of brooding here alone;
come out to the field again, love,"
I'll place his hand under my heart
to feel the generations,

and he will tell me I'm like Grandma Sarah,
a late bloomer — but special.

Sisters
by Rosa Felsenburg Kaplan

Married to one man
Could Rachel and Leah
Be sisters still?

She had brushed her hair
And tamed the darkness
With a bedtime story.
The feel of the strokes on her hair
Said, "Rachel you are beautiful."
The trusting head on her shoulder
Said, "Leah, I love you."

They played with their brothers
And had a fierce family loyalty,
But sometimes they had to admit
That they believed women
Understood women
In ways men never possibly could.
Sometimes they would wonder
Whether the man they would love
Might not be different
And know how they felt.

She shed a tear
Behind her veil
When he called her Rachel.
But his joy in his young manhood
Blue and purple licking flames
The orange roar,
The gushing river,
The quiet glowing embers afterwards
Filled her with gratitude.

By day, Rachel would ask
About the night's events.
Now, to quell her own
Fear of the light,
Leah told of waving water anemones,
Of darting tongues of barnacles,
Of opening and shutting shells,
Of waves and waves of ocean
And of quiet shore.

That he would call her Rachel
Each time his joy hit a crescendo
And that his doing so
Would quell her flames a little,
Not to hurt Rachel
She kept her secret.

Like a pomegranate blossom
She had moved on slender branches.
Rachel watched
The calyx grow, the blossom shrivel
The fruit ripe, orange red . . .
The infant at her breast,
Mother and child at peace . . .
Leah, once set aside, a queen.

The veil barely contained
Her joy and passion
As Rachel ended the seventh circle.
Jacob was a radiant groom,
The years of service ended,
The treasure his.

She sang as she readied herself
To meet her lover
The song of Leah's passion in her ear.

On the bridal bed,
As his hands moved over hair
Shoulders, breasts, thighs
His touch said, "Rachel, you are beautiful,"
And his words, "Rachel, I love you."

While he handled her tenderly
Like Phoenician glass,
The long awaited treasure,
Rachel struggled to feel
The flames of love
The waves of passion,
The melting together with him
Of which Leah had told.

He feared to hurt her,
Talked tenderly,
He wished to please her in every way
But in the one for which she waited
That he take his pleasure in her
Losing himself in his own passion,
Rousing his flame in her.
Alone, Rachel shed a tear,
As she brushed her hair,
Repeating, "Rachel, you are beautiful."

Like a pomegranate blossom,
She moved on slender stalk
Season after season.
The blossom never shriveled
The calyx never thickened,
Year after year,
He spanned her waist with ease.
Year after year,
He loved her tenderly,
Delicately,
Attentively.

Once, as he caressed her shoulders,
Breasts, thighs
Treasuring her beauty,
She burst out,
"Give me children or I am dead!"

Anger, twice seven years caged,
Burst.
"Did not the years of my bride service
Tell you I love you?
And my devotion now?"

The gentle strokes grew rough
He filled her emptiness with rage.
Strong, violent.
With cries of, "Leah!"

The blossom shriveled,
The calyx became swollen
Grew lumpy.
She dreaded each morning
And the day of her confinement,
Lacking the ease of Leah's motherhood.

On the road near Bethlehem,
Jacob wept.
"She was a woman made to be treasured, loved,
Not to bear children.
To be a child, a sister,
Not a man's wife,"
Said Leah.

Princess Michal's Song
by Rosalind Darrow

Here in the garden
Sit David and I
Weaving a garland
Of cob-webs and dew
David is telling his
Love in a song
And the music is sweet
And the words are not true.

David is born with
The wanderer's curse
That yearns toward the desert
And looks to the skies —
But David has taken
My face in his hands
And presses his lips
Upon each of my eyes.

Here in the garden
Sit David and I
close by the fountain,
With hands woven tight.
Evening will take him
Away to the hills
And I shall weave
Garlands alone in the night.

1951, United States.

Michal
by Rachel Blaustein

*And Michal, Saul's daughter, loved David —
and she despised him in her heart.*

Though years divide, we're sisters yet;
Your vineyard stands though weeds invade;
Still tinkle anklet, amulet;
Your red silk garment does not fade.

By a small window still you stand,
Proud, but a death within your eyes.
My sister, I can understand —
Who also love whom I despise.

1927, Israel.
Translated from Hebrew by Robert Friend

Amol Iz Geven

Brushing
by Madeline Tiger

"Once there lived side by side/ Two little maids,
Always dressed just alike/ Hair down in braids . . ."

Your arrival was always with cashews,
hugs, baggage; you'd unpin your hat,
lift back the veil, sigh, lean back,
lift the hat off, say "Haaaa"

In the evening, there was talk
about New York, tenants, rentals,
your friends in the park . . .
the pigeons ate right out of your hands

Your trip would have been tiring,
uneventful: more sighing,
Mother would go for "tea," I'd be sent
upstairs, my room suddenly

full of strange lingerie and brushes,
I'd rush — pajamas, and under the covers
before I'm too late for your arrival,
now! mine, you'd change: billowing and pillowy

you'd fill everywhere with a command
the voice calling me —
a smell of must, unfolding, an old
suitcase, closed, and dark

couches; a smell of things washed
long ago, body creases, the damp
under your straps, your huge corset,
the big brassiere like a harness,

the dark of your armpits. Later
I will crawl in there, I can be sure
you will invite me
I will be hiding

from enemies and hungry witches,
but now, in your long slips,
in your loose largeness, you lift
those great arms, the fat

hanging, and heave
your hands to your hair,
hand over hand, pulling pin
after pin, those grey wire tricks

that keep you neat, that hold you, I —
I hold my breath watching as the hair
comes down, as if out of the braids in
your songs, the braids hanging down

under "bonnets," the girls in your songs
wandering "by the garden path" down
to the old well and secrets, "secrets
they tell . . ." I reach you the brush and

I watch as your grey hair floats
to the tune of   hush hush   the
hushing strokes, over the bed, over the carpet
over and over, and you talking stories of

hayrides and wine-sipping, brothers and sisters
and mothers and milk, the nuns and the ocean,
the steamship, the birthday, the crossing,
the babies, the sweatshop, my father, you stroking

hush and I'm rocking in down and I'm hearing again
how you came here and worked and your son was so good to you BRUSH
and your grey hair is shining all over my bedroom, BRUSH, and your
warm arms are light in the light of the stories this evening you're

tireless brushing away the tight pull and you tell me of the days
(I smell something folded and under and musty and old,
of ovens and waiting and "humba" the swing on the back porch
and yeasty, to be savored, and used; something unused, and spoken for)

he said you were beautiful, you tell me again — he wanted to
comb your long hair
and you tell me how thick it was then when he went to college
(to me it is thicker than anything human), and long; it reminds me of
Europe, of haystacks, of kitchens and rushes of language. You invite me

to feel it, I touch it, I shrink back under the covers. You tell me
again, tossing and laughing — how good and how thick it is, still,
(with the last brush strokes) you still have your beauty,
you climb into bed with me, gowned, lemon-scented, I

sink in your bosom
I dissolve in an ocean of grey
I dream about somebody
brushing and combing us

Names
by Ruth Daigon

Sunday nights at 7, he's here.
Sits at the kitchen table.
Picks the largest apple in the bowl.
And with something older than patience,
he begins the silent, ritual peeling.
His knife makes a quick incision
back into the past.
We sit as they sat long ago,
waiting for the apples to be stripped,
cored, sprinkled with cinnamon.
He scrapes away the soft spots,
making the fruit perfect
while we wind each spiral
through our fingers
and inhale the fragrance
of familiar names.
Noah   words shooting
from the sharp edge of his tongue,
David   swimming deep enough to drown,
Riva   smiles crackling like parchment,
Sonya, Sam, Reuben, Gitel.
Names
heavy with old weather.
Names
calling like train whistles in the dark.
Names
smelling of strange earth
where they have been
and gone from
and we will never know
as we watch our uncle peeling back
the layers of our lives.

First published in Poet Lore, *1989.*

Braids
by Layle Silbert

Friday morning
I braid my hair
in front of the mirror
cannot see behind my head
think of braids
I might have made
on a Friday morning
kneading dough
separating it into strands
& braiding them
into a crown
round as a rose
as only our village did
for Sabbath bread
the whole world would know
here is a challah from Tels
taste it

First published in Midstream, *1989.*

Gey Klap Dem Kop In Vant
by Mildred Brenner Pollner

"Go bang you head against the wall!"
she would say to me,
whenever I asked
"What should I do now?"

"Gey klap dem kop in vant!"
her form of endearment
not generally noted
in childrearing manuals!

And I would laugh and sing
and dance away,
for her words were all wise,
her pronouncements
music to my ears!

Saul's Hammer
by Dina Elenbogen

Today it matters, that I hold
this hammer in my fist, that maybe
fifty years ago you held this hammer
in your fist, that I know this only
because your name is engraved in the metal.

So I call this hammer Saul, and Saul
hangs calendars, cards, and baskets
of bananas, oranges, and onions.
That Saul escaped Russia, was a Socialist, fixed teeth,
had the purest white hair at the end of his life—

these are only stories; that you died
when my mother's belly was full.
There are other things
I would have never asked you;
how you felt when you saw the first

buds on a tree, or the last,
that you never had time to notice
the blossoming and the dying
and what that meant.

Saul Katzenellenbogen
1877–1953

First printed in Tomorrow Magazine, *Chicago, 1988.*

Maggid
by Marge Piercy

The courage to let go of the door, the handle.
The courage to shed the familiar walls whose very
stains and leaks are comfortable as the little moles
of the upper arm; stains that recall a feast,
a child's naughtiness, a loud blattering storm
that slapped the roof hard, pouring through.

The courage to abandon the graves dug into the hill,
the small bones of children and the brittle bones
of the old whose marrow hunger had stolen;
the courage to desert the tree planted and only
begun to bear; the riverside where promises were
shaped; the street where their empty pots were broken.

The courage to leave the place whose language you learned
as early as your own, whose customs however dangerous or demeaning, bind you like a halter
you have learned to pull inside, to move your load;
the land fertile with the blood spilled on it;
the roads mapped and annotated for survival.

The courage to walk out of the pain that is known
into the pain that cannot be imagined,
mapless, walking into the wilderness, going
barefoot with a canteen into the desert;
stuffed in the stinking hold of a rotting ship
sailing off the map into dragons' mouths.

Cathay, India, Siberia, *goldeneh medina*,
leaving bodies by the way like abandoned treasure.
So they walked out of Egypt. So they bribed their way
out of Russia under loads of straw; so they steamed
out of the blood smoking charnelhouse of Europe
on overloaded freighters forbidden all ports—

out of pain into death or freedom or a different
painful dignity, into squalor and politics.
We Jews are all born of wanderers, with shoes
under our pillows and a memory of blood that is ours
raining down. We honor only those Jews who changed
tonight, those who chose the desert over bondage,

who walked into the strange and became strangers
and gave birth to children who could look down
on them standing on their shoulders for having
been slaves. We honor those who let go of every-
thing but freedom, who ran, who revolted, who fought,
who became other by saving themselves.

First published in Available Light, *Knopf, 1988.*

Farewell Earth
by Peninnah Braude

How I love to breathe the air of you
(Polluted and filthy though it be!)
How I love to move my body in the space of you, Earth
Forming patterns and designs,
Displacing space with me   displacing me with space
And sometimes I practice my tight-rope walking!
Mostly, I love to feel the air filter through my fingers.
But all this will cease soon for I shall die.
Yes, I shall surely die.
And when I lie in the dust
No poppies, please, around my grave,
No nightingales or Psalms.
Just silence. S i l e n c e .
Silentium mundi
And in the still night
When only the moon rages through the clouds
Perhaps someone will remember me, smile, and drop a tear.
One tear.
One tear.
One.

Rozhinkes Mit Mandlen
by Irene Javors

Mamushka,
it has been so long
since we have spoken,
Remember,
how we sat in air cooled
movie houses
on warm summer afternoons
in July.
I would translate
the dialogue
so that
you would understand
the story.
Often,
you would mumble
to me
in Russian-Yiddish
of cossacks
and
pogroms,
and tears would well up
in your eyes.
I would take hold
of
your hand
and
say, "let's have a Good Humor,"
and
off we'd go
in search of
popsicle sticks.
In the morning,
you always
read

The Forward
and
argued with the
ghosts
of your comrades.
I'd hear you speak,
with great conviction,
of how Czar Nicholas
deserved everything
that happened to him.
At the table, you would sip tea
out of a glass
that you held
in your right hand
while
simultaneously
taking a bite
from a small sugar cube
that sat poised between
thumb and forefinger
of your left hand.
This delicate balance between
glass and cube
seemed quite
an
achievement to me.
a greater mystery involved
your ability to hold such
a hot glass without getting burned.
You'd laugh and say,
   "It was so cold in Russia
   that I learned to hold
   fire in my palms."
Sometimes, you'd forget to speak to me
in English
and you'd talk in Russian,
expecting me to answer you.
I would say, "I don't understand."

You would answer, "No, you are the only one who does
    understand."
Then, you'd get a strange look
in your dark eyes
and
hold me close to you.
When you seemed to see things
that I did not,
you would speak of distant places
with exotic names,
Baku,
Ararat,
Rostov on the Don,
and
of mysterious doings
in the dark of the night,
You smelled of farina
and
old newspapers.
You had an ivory comb
that you delicately ran
through your wavy
white hair.
You'd tell me secrets
about
Russia,
the Revolution,
and
your brother whom you loved so very much.
You'd curse at Stalin
and warn me
about
tyrants
who would steal our souls
if they could.
I would imitate your accent
and
pretend that I was a bohemian
who
presided over a salon
in Brighton Beach.

Grandma,
I'm all grown up now,
I don't sing your labor songs
and
I have forgotten the words to your
beloved *Internationale*.
At night,
As I fall asleep,
I hear you
singing a lullaby
of raisins and almonds.
I imagine you sitting
by the window
watching for signs of spring.
So many years have passed,
all that remains is memory
and your familiar voice
that speaks to me
in dreams.
Remember our promise to each other.
We agreed
that
when the Revolution comes
we will make certain
that
everyone eats strawberries
and
dances in the moonlight.
In this paradise
    of
freedom,
we will rejoice
in our reunion.
Until then,
I say,
to you,
with love,
das vedonya, tovarish.
Goodbye, dear friend.

My Next Door Neighbor
by Mindy Rinkewich

My old neighbor isn't in the apartment any more
Her niece has lived there for a year, two . . .
But I have a photograph of her aunt as a young lady
How dignified, how grown-up, how elegant.
That photograph
talks:
— I'm not just some snapshot
— I'm a portrait
— They don't make them like me any more
— I'm a portrait from portrait-land
— That land is no more
Those who plied that trade
Have already been working the other side a long time.

Her niece makes a living in the rag business
She is a fashion forecaster
A very contemporary profession
She began by giving the apartment a fresh coat of paint
She refurnished it in an up-to-date manner
As to her great aunt's family pictures
Into the garbage
All, all of it
Put out with the garbage downstairs.

A complete album
Several envelopes
Even the one marked, "For Uncle Harry".
Even, dear God,
Her great great grandfather
lost in thought on a road in Mlave
Even the portrait of her aunt as a young lady
Dolléd up like a star in an evening gown with real pearls.

Against this girl I don't have any big complaints
She is a forecaster of fashions yet to come in the world
I am a reminder of fashions no longer of this world
The world itself consists of two kinds of people:
Those who throw away old pictures
And those who pick them up.

From a cycle of Yiddish poems entitled "Di Neksdorike."

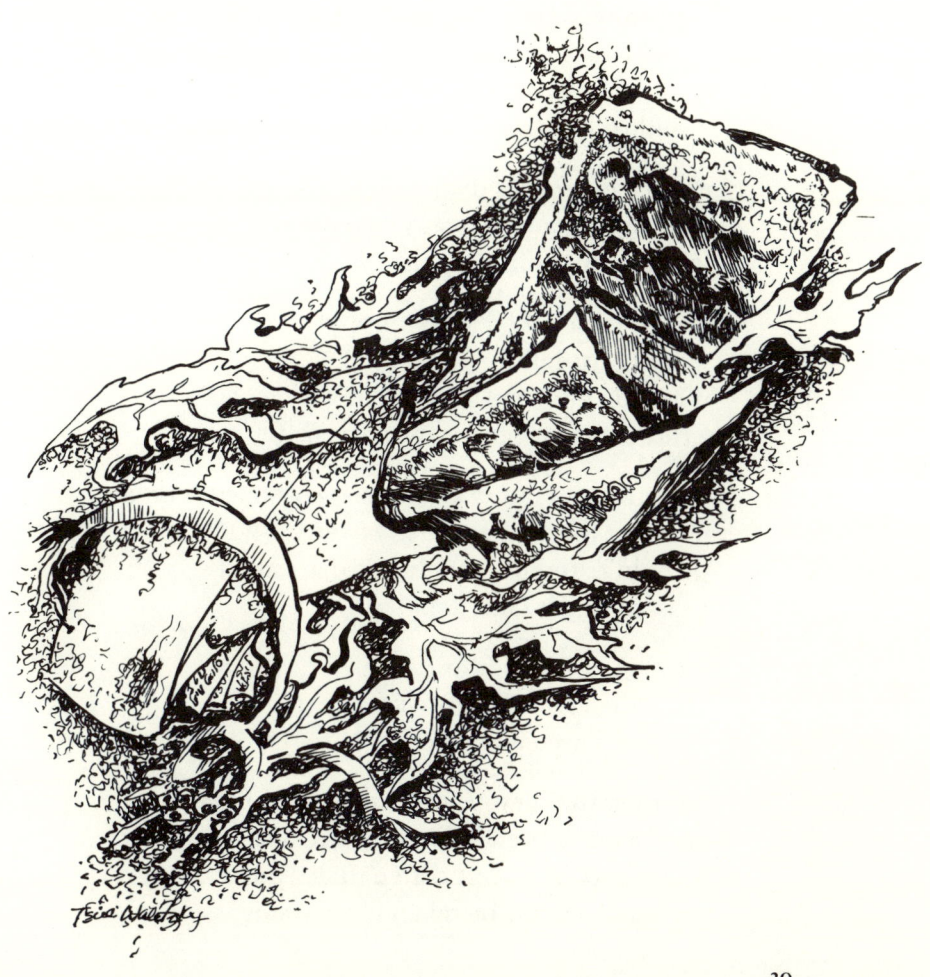

Boiled Wine
by Lucy Cohen Schmeidler

My brother's father-in-law kept boiled wine
to serve to guests, Jews like himself—
but maybe, G-d forbid, not Sabbath-keeping
(and thus, in some respects, like *goyim*).

The Law is clear:
    plain wine is for ourselves, for celebrations
    and toasts among our own. We may not drink it
    with those who worship falseness,
    and those who pour libations to strange gods.

Plain wine makes distinctions: us and other;
marriages permitted and forbidden.
It keeps our children ours.

Boiled wine's a friendly puppy
wagging its tail for everyone;
it guards no fence around the Law.
(And yet, you cannot taste the difference.)

my brother's father-in-law served boiled wine,
marking his guests as maybe out-of-bounds.
(It didn't stop his daughter's marriage.)
I tasted insult, and kept still.

How shall I pass it on?
I am a Jew, a woman, writer, person;
my peers are everywhere.

Keeping the Law, I walk among the nations,
and cast my friendship where it will.
I serve not wine but coffee to my guests, and pray
my children not be taken for my sins.

They Did Not Build Wings For Them
by Irena Klepfisz

they did not build wings for them
the unmarried aunts; instead they
crammed them into old maids' rooms
or placed them as nannies with
the younger children: mostly they
ate in the kitchen, but sometimes
were permitted to dine with the family
for which they were grateful and
smiled graciously as the food was passed.
they would eat slowly never filling
their plates and their hearts would
sink at the evening's end when it was
time to retreat into an upstairs corner.

but there were some who did not smile
who never wished to be grafted on
the bursting houses. these few remained
indifferent to the family gatherings
preferring the aloneness of their small rooms
which they decorated with odd objects
found on long walks. they collected
bird feathers and skulls unafraid to clean
them to whiteness; stones which resembled
humped bears or the more common tiger and
wolf; dried leaves whose brilliant colors
never faded; pieces of wood still covered
with fresh moss and earth which retained
their moisture and continued flourishing.
these they placed by their dresser mirror
in arrangements reminiscent of secret rites
or hung over delicate watercolors of unruly
trees whose branches were about to snap
with the wind.

it happened sometimes, that among these
one would venture even further. periodically
would be heard vague tales of a woman
withdrawn and inaccessible suddenly disappearing
one autumn night leaving her room bare
of herself. women gossiped about a man.
but eventually word would come back
she had moved north to the ocean and lived
alone.   she was still collecting.
but now her house was filled with crab
and lobster shells; discolored claws
which looked like grinning south american
parrots trapped in fish nets decorated
the walls; skulls of unidentifiable
creatures were arranged in geometric patterns
and soft reeds in tall green bottles
lined the window sills.   one room
in the back with totally bare walls
was a workshop.   here she sorted colored
shells and pasted them on wooden boards
in the shape of common flowers.   these she sold
without sentiment.

such a one might also disappear inland.
rumor would claim she had travelled in
men's clothing.   two years later it would
be reported she had settled in the woods
on some cleared land.   she ran a small farm
mainly for supplying herself with food
and wore strangely patched dresses and shawls
of oddly matched materials.   but aloneness
was her real distinction.   the house was neat
and the pantry full.   seascapes and pastoral
scenes hung on the walls.   the garden was
well kept and the flower beds clearly defined
by color: red   yellow   blue.   in the woods
five miles from the house she had an orchard

here she secretly grafted and crossed varieties
creating singular fruit of shades and scents
never thought possible.   her experiments rarely
failed and each spring she waited eagerly to see
what new forms would hang from the trees.
here the world was a passionate place and she
would visit it at night baring her breasts
to the moon.

First published in Different Enclosures: The Poetry and Prose of Irena Klepfisz, *Onlywomen Press, 1985.*

Rosie
by Nicole Lieberman

She tosses bread to them
and like the pigeons
she doesn't know
if Monday breaks with dawn
or Saturday.
She thinks she's sixty-two
or maybe older.
She knows for certain
her brown hair turned gray.

Her world is stacked
inside a cart
from the Red Apple.
She wears a plastic bag
and lost her comb.
When people stare
she holds her hand out, yelling:
"You gonna give me change
or take me home?"

She found a watch and
traded it for men's shoes.
Too big, she stuffed them
with the *Times*
to make them fit.
They make her shuffle
and they give her blisters;
at night she puts on bandages
of spit.

Sometimes she thinks of
when she had pajamas —
clean sheets —
and pillows —
and a bed.
And when her husband left her
she was glad:
he beat her with his fists.
One time she bled.

Maybe she saw it in the movies —
maybe she dreamt it —
did she have a husband?
Was he dead?
She likes the guy who
works the night-shift
at the deli;
he gives her ends
from cold-cuts. And stale bread.

The Beggar in the Subway
by Helen Papell

The subway beggar crouches against the token booth
like a bird pushed to a jetty by a sea of oil.
My dead mother's voice says "Share your Sabbath,"
And I remember a Friday rain
When a beggar's fingers thrust like sandpiper's stilts
into a garbage can in front of our tenement.

She said to him "Come, eat with us. What horizons
do you wander, that you are an orphan on Sabbath?"
He babbled of a sky so close to the sea
that a cloud pulled flowers from the waves,
And when I demanded proof   he gave me a starfish
curled toward the Sabbath candles
like petals opening a daisy to sun.

The subway beggar's fingers, mossed with tar,
Lift a paper cup and wait for a wave to feed him.
I drop several coins and flee
to my apartment with three locks on the door,
Unable to explain to my dead mother
That houses of the rich now crowd their stilts
at the edge of the sea,
Unable to explain the journey I have traveled
That I dare tell a beggar, in this Friday rain,
to look for Sabbath inside the aquarium windows
of a public shelter.

First published in Visions, *1985.*

Subway Song
by Lucy Cohen Schmeidler

big black man hugging the subway pole
sings to himself, not loud but audibly,
parts of a song
and then just humming —
crazy or not, it makes no difference —
melody from his soul
that settles into my bones
until I want to harmonize

(but I, small white woman,
keep my mouth closed
and my eyes elsewhere)

Poetry
by Annette Bialik Harchik

My grandfather Pesach hung himself
one spring day in Poland.
He first worked wheatfields,
then sold grain, later wood.
Unsuccessful with his lumberyard in Tuliszkow
he turned from timber to textiles
selling cloth among his Christian neighbors.
He found the cruelty around him too oppressive,
his rural poverty too stark,
his intellectual aspirations too elusive.
He spun his dreams in another world.
He wrote his poetry in Hebrew.

My father, Abram, eldest of six,
was orphaned at age twelve.
Apprenticed to a Kolo tailor,
he turned to a socialist movement
in hope of transcending his poverty.
He looked to democratic methods,
the dignity of love
as answers to provincial hatreds.
A quintessential survivor —
his humble values clear:
love of life, people, justice.
He wrote his poetry in Yiddish.

I write too; an only child, female,
a triumphant growth despite genocide.
Having spent diverse amounts of time
coming of age in New York City,
I went off to college, then graduate studies,
to meet head on
our own social inequalities.
In the U.S. of A. there are many forms of poverty
not all easily identifiable.

I teach young children and
try to build a better world.
I write my poetry in English.

Three generations
unpublished poets
each not knowing the language of the other.

Jabotinsky Street
by Dina Elenbogen

for Robert Friend

For the man who nurses
twelve cats, one without claws,
one speechless, one with tunnel vision,
I bring pomegranates from the market
on Ben Yehuda Street, although
last month they were ripe on the tree
in front of my lover's house.

I bring him these fruits for tomorrow
when I will already be on my way
to another country.
Each seed is a blessing.
I try to believe each seed
is another year of his life.

His Arab house keeper serves us fish soup.
Bread is constantly popping from the toaster.
We critique the flavor of the seasoning,
compare it with last month's stew,
last month, when my skin wasn't so brown
when the wine didn't spin my head so,
when I wasn't so close to the border.

Between the soup and sherbet
we critique my poems, my words
which have become his jewels, this man
who has taken in another cat this month,
without a tail, with a loud cry,
as I have taken in a new lover,
a Moroccan without manners.

We finish the game of solitaire
he began before I arrived. He keeps
turning up the ace of spades,
the card of death, says it is always falling
from his neighbor's balcony, lands on his lawn,
something he stumbles past
on his way to collect the mail.

The oldest cat lands on the bookshelf.
His limbs heal in this room
where Martin Buber once stored
his books, where my friend collects
the words of three generations, writes
the words of two countries,
and gives me black tea

as I gather the fallen pomegranate seeds
plant them in a pot outside his window and pray
things will not stop blooming.

Jerusalem, 1985
First published in prairie schooner *September, 1989*

Growing Up
by Dina Elenbogen

for Beryl

i

I packed all those important pieces
of the past in a box before I left.
Besides your boots that I stole
from your closet, the only picture
of you I have was taken
when I was five and you were seven.
For once, the sun wasn't in our eyes.

We were standing in the living
room, the old living room
when we still had the gray carpet
with orange juice stains.
I'm not sure anymore who spilled
it. We passed the blame back and forth
like an old doll.

In the picture we were dressed
like twins. Behind us, a window
where evening became gray like the carpet.
Next to me was mom's vase with houses
painted on of a land we only dreamed of.

The dried weeds growing out of
our Promised Land were taller than both of us.
It must have been autumn.
Our bangs were cut unevenly and we were
wearing our Israeli blouses with red
white and blue embroidery around the neck,
our hands tightly joined.

ii

I remember almost ten years later
we sat on a bench overlooking
the rolling gold and green of Tzvat,
birthplace of the kabbalah.
What we shared in palms that didn't touch
was a heaviness that spread in our hearts.

After the Mediterranean sun dried water
from our faces, I saw the long white beard
of a man who watched us with a wisdom
I had searched for. I imagined the mystics
centuries ago, on their knees gathering sparks,
their eyes tired from watching for G-d.

I wanted to ask for some extra sparks
he might have hidden in his pocket.
Instead we walked through the colony,
legs suddenly stronger.
We peered into ancient temples
collected hand painted vases.

You bought me a ring made out of black
onyx, like one that you had,
rings that have wrapped our fingers
through all these years of growing
and falling back.

Sister Prophecy: A Gift for Bonita's 32nd Birthday
by Celia Y. Weisman

1961

Round bellied sisters
pose tummy to tummy
daddy takes the snapshot.

She's taller
    older
        more controlled.

I'm 5
she's 7
and hey, it's summer!

I wipe my nose on her frilly pink swim-suit
and we're daddy's bathing beauties posing in
backyard sun.

1986

She and I danced through young womanhood
sweating and exploring
writing and chanting
loving and hurting
dreaming.

She and I fought Amazon battles.
Moved apart.
Forgot the contents of each other's dresser drawers.
Stopped saying "I love you" with each phone conversation's
   end.
The blood bond weakened, and daddy could no longer catch
his two bathing beauties in a single frame.

Now in our thirties, we wonder.
Are we complete enough?
Strong enough?
Ourselves enough?
Are we finished being roof-top gypsies?
Have we had enough freedom?
Dare we carry the moon in our bellies?
There is only one moon
and two sisters.

1991

Round bellied sisters
pose tummy to tummy.
One moon inside both of us now.

That Your Life May Be Long

Song for My Father
by S. Ben-Tov

Peace, the hour
when doves crowd the top of the thicket,
and across the tiles of the yard
a few dry leaves are blown
as stars come out:
the gate creaks;
on the far hill a coyote wails.
The words of our songs
come back to you like roads in the dusk:
the red dirt road,
the locked gate we climb over,
the lights of the kibbutz
waiting in the bare hall
where memories sit down together.
The secret, so clear now:
peace has always
shadowed these fields
at this hour
for anyone who walked in them;
who walked on home
toward the lights winking out
in the children's house,
and the steady lamp
shining from the watchtower.
The words of our poets
come back to you like songs:

my heart is straight

as a blade of grass

among the grasses of the field.

From the long poem "During Ceasefire," *first published in* During Ceasefire, *by Sharona Ben-Tov. Reprinted by permission of Harper & Row, Publishers, Inc. © 1985 by Sharona Ben-Tov.*

Fathers
by Cecile L. Martindale

My father would sing to me
And, as children assume
Whatever delights
Is due them,
I gave no thought
To fathers who do not sing,
Or name the stars,
Or turn a leaf and guide small fingers
To the Braille of the underside.

The Rock
by Natalie R. Sheffler

My father was the silence that we ate
like the dessert of a last birthday,
as secret as crumbs without bread.

If I had grabbed leftovers from his plate,
would he have breathed
without breaking a word?

To find him, I had to pull hazel from his eyes,
sober, sober man,
and guess the wrinkles weren't crying.

He took me to be the fisherman in his boat,
to pass sandwiches to worms
until the water was shade.
Sunburn puffed his skin.

Now we could suck the air, not quite
longing to belong. We were delighted
that the ocean, the clouds, the fish were unaware
of pawned rings
or gambling for food,
ulcerated years, the swelled tongue
of a man a little afraid of living.

Once he hit me, once I saw him cry,
and once I held his trembling
on my arm when I married in the tent of his home.

On the water, in the boat, fishing, he didn't speak
to the open world;

he lowered his voice so the neighbors couldn't hear,
his silence the rock inside the stone.

Momma Remembers
by Elaine Mitchell

In Zerdover
I couldn't go
to school. I was a girl.
I danced to the window
of the little shul
where the boys' heads nodding
sent their curls bobbing,
the yardstick cracking the tune.
On the edge of the desk,
on the back of the hand.
I recited along with them.

We stored our food
in an unheated room

where Fanny and I peeled
potatoes. Momma plucked chickens
in the back yard, her wig slipping
over one ear. Her fuzzy head
stirred a breeze as she worked.
The feathers waltzed with the wind.
Cut off our long hair after we married?
Brown braids tossed wildly. NO.
Peelings polkaed down to the dirt floor.
Our bare toes wouldn't stop wriggling.

In America
my sisters said   Go to school;
you're just ten. NO.   I'd work,
like them. Each morning I danced
uptown.   A mile from Hester Street
to Nemo on Astor Place.   Sewed steel
stays into ladies' corsets.   Rib
to thigh ten hours a day, six days
a week. My legs would ache to stretch
and kick.   The union got started. The girls
were afraid.   I joined, walked the picket
line.   People laughed at women on strike.
My friend Rose and I, you know her,
made up a song we whispered at our
machines, bent over like mothers
over their baby:
Foot on the treadle
won't rock the cradle.

In night school
I couldn't sit still, kept
falling asleep.   And my teacher
was handsome as Valentino.   Stayed
after class to go over my lessons,
took me dancing too.   He wanted
to marry a greenhorn like me.

I stopped going to class,
went out only with landsmen.
They all wanted to marry me.
I wanted to go on dancing.

Your father's sisters —
I knew them from Zerdover —
sent him to visit when he arrived.
A quiet man.   So good-looking.   Redhead,
like you.   He kept coming back.
Everyone said he'd make a good
husband.   But he didn't know how
to dance.   Too busy with socialist
meetings.   My sisters said
Grab him.   Grab him.

I remember a dream I had
after we were married.   They come
for me in an open wagon.   Polish soldiers.
They come to take me away.   I yell
for help. I beg on my knees.   They
laugh, pick me up, throw me in
with the others.   I reach out
my arms, screaming to Momma.
JUMP, Momma yells, JUMP.
The horses start up the road
leaving town.   She stretches
her arms to catch me.
JUMP.   JUMP.

What do you do?
I ask, caught at last.

I wake up.

The Depression
by Dina Elenbogen

i

Bees celebrate Indian Summer
flying in and out of the window.
It's the beginning of the month
and the kitchen is almost empty.
We've been eating dark tuna all week.

Even the cat can't stand the heat.
She sniffs the floor for crumbs
and catches bees in her mouth until they go mad
or die. Their relatives pay no attention to
history, but it's too hot to close
the window with potatoes baking in the oven.

A friend once told me a person could live
on potatoes only if he ate enough of them.
But my friend wore a striped suit and shiny shoes
into Chicago every morning and added up
other people's bills. I laughed. Potatoes.
I still laugh.

It's easy to forget and buy jugs of wine
and shiny knives that are guaranteed
to cut through almost anything. It's easy
to forget until thunder rattles the windows
and the lights flicker and go out.

In the morning the paper is too wet
to read. It is easier to live outside
the world, ignore the bills in the mail,
hide in the darkness of shadows.

ii

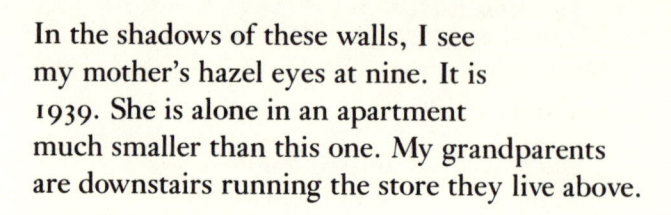

In the shadows of these walls, I see
my mother's hazel eyes at nine. It is
1939. She is alone in an apartment
much smaller than this one. My grandparents
are downstairs running the store they live above.

Her brothers and sisters are out with friends.
Dinner will be late tonight.
After a while hunger just goes away. My mother
watches the potatoes browning in the oven.
The warmth feels good.

It isn't always this lonely. At night
there are eight of them sleeping across
the living room floor. My grandmother is too tired
to yell about my mother's only doll who emigrated
to the roof, or the dead field mouse the cat
brought home. No one took it away.

It is almost winter
so everyone will sleep close tonight
as if there were room for some sort of love.
Next week my grandfather will get more wood.
There is no room to worry about saving
on a crowded floor, except in the crevices
of the wall where the cat hid the other half
of the mouse for breakfast.

iii

My mother never worried about the past.
She worried about sleeping through the night
without the sound of someone
else's dreams keeping her awake.
Of course there were dreams.
At night they flew above my mother's head
and she wrote them down on pieces of paper.

Late in the afternoon, while other families
sat down to eat, she threw the pieces
of paper inside the last sparks of fire.
At night, when she slept, they flew
out the chimney and danced
all over Chicago.

Her dreams didn't leave.
When I was a child she would rock me in her lap
and read me stories about Adam and Eve,
how the world began. She fed pieces
of the past to me every night and they grew
in my sleep.

I remember how Adam cried on his first day
on earth when suddenly it got dark.
He thought G-D was taking the world away from him.
Adam didn't know the sun would come back
if he closed his eyes and rested.

the way my mother closed her eyes
and waited for the space to breathe,
the way I close my eyes and wait for the lights
to come back on.

First published in Rhino, *1988.*

Learning Bones
by Rhina P. Espaillat

I'm learning bones to please my father's ghost.
Cranium, Maxilla — he knew them all
and loved to reel them off, each Latin name
sonorous and ornate, as from a tongue
speaking the nineteenth century. He'd boast —
his only vanity — total recall:
Mandibula, Clavicula — and not
one out of place, named wrongly, or forgot,
although learned long ago, when he was young.
Useless for me to argue that "breastbone"
is really just as good and quite the same
as Sternum; on that point, he became stone.

Gospelled by my own time, I worshipped use:
What use was it, I gibed, to learn by heart,
in a dead language, static part by part?
Better to know the function of the glands,
for instance (which I knew he did not know),
the mind's evasions, or the work of dreams.

He didn't like my century: obtuse,
almost, to change, he couldn't trust what seems;
he wanted things to *be*, and to be there
forever in their place, like arms and hands.
Humerus, Radius, Ulna do not flow
beyond mind's grasp like impulse or nightmare.
He liked the rational, the decent look
of bones in place, holding the flesh upright
as bones do — as they seem to, in his book.

When Latin failed him, and the torment came
that numbered and wrenched his bones as on a rack,
he learned the flow of nightmare into night.

The journey he took up has no returning,
and no soft speech will bring soft answer back,
but (clumsy, slow Aeneas!) I am learning
Ilium, Ischium, Femura — long prayer
always descending earthward, rung by rung —
Fibula, Metatarsus — to the ground
in whose disorder lies that careful man.

Pious at last, I pray his sleep is sound.
We make amends in any way we can.

First published in Plains Poetry Journal, *1987.*

Six O'Clock News
by Ruth Daigon

At six o'clock, my mother
always listened to the news
and groaned.
She was a small woman —
ninety-six pounds,
but her body was
a vast burial ground
for all the victims of
floods, revolutions, wars,
each groan another corpse
entering her body.
I'd fold the wash
as she stood ironing —
every stroke a preparation
for the burial,
a straightening of limbs,
a smoothing of features,
a final act of love.

First published in Learning Not to Kill You, *Selkirk Press, 1976.*

1932
by Lynn Saul

Harry Saul wraps the leather strap of the *tefillin* box around his arm
Harry Saul recites his prayers next to his bedroom window
watches snow layering the branches of the sycamores outside his window
Harry Saul prays the way his father and his grandfather prayed
on winter mornings in Lithuania

although here Harry Saul is a merchant of Michelin tires
he lets his son wear the Michelin Man suit
lets his son parade around the streets of East Liberty
advertising Michelin tires
like some fat rubber tire man I saw just last week
marching down Stone Avenue in Tucson Arizona

and he lets his daughter hitchhike with her girlfriend
hitchhike across the continent like any young man might
also he has taught his daughter Torah, he has let her go to college

and here on a snowy January day Harry Saul is in his bedroom praying
and his wife has just walked downstairs to make the morning oatmeal and coffee
and there asleep in Harry Saul's favorite wing chair is a man
normally we might call him a burglar
he just came in off the streets for a warm place to sit

it's a January morning, there is snow on the sycamores
Harry Saul's wife is surprised, she's afraid, the man is large, and he happens to be black
he's asleep in his overcoat, his hands are nestled in its torn pockets

Harry's wife goes upstairs, she doesn't scream, she asks her
   husband what to do
Harry Saul tells his wife he is praying the way
his father and his grandfather prayed in Lithuania, he tells her
to leave him alone, so she walks downstairs
she walks past the man sleeping in her husband's wing chair

she thinks of her son, overheating in the tire suit
she thinks of her daughter, taking rides from strangers in
   Montana
she walks to the kitchen without waking the man
she makes the man oatmeal and coffee.

1940
by Madeline Tiger

   i hated
   mother's tennis dress
   she had fat legs
   when she wore it
   she couldn't hear
   a thing i said
   when she put it on
   she was a large knee
   a tight jawbone
   she had no ears
   suddenly her eyes
   blew away
   like the white balls

   the raquet, arm and all,
   moved like
   my German clown
   my wind-up doll

   First published in Corduroy. *1973*

Belonging
by Layle Silbert

my father belonged
first to his native place
in America he belonged
where he lived
his true being belonged
in Israel even before
it was born
he made speeches
filled with passion & belief

on the streets of Jerusalem
is that my father
sniffing the holy air
in a Tel Aviv cafe
confronting the Knesset
on a stroll in the old city?

until he died
he was afraid to go
where he belonged
the most

First published in Jewish Frontier, *1985.*

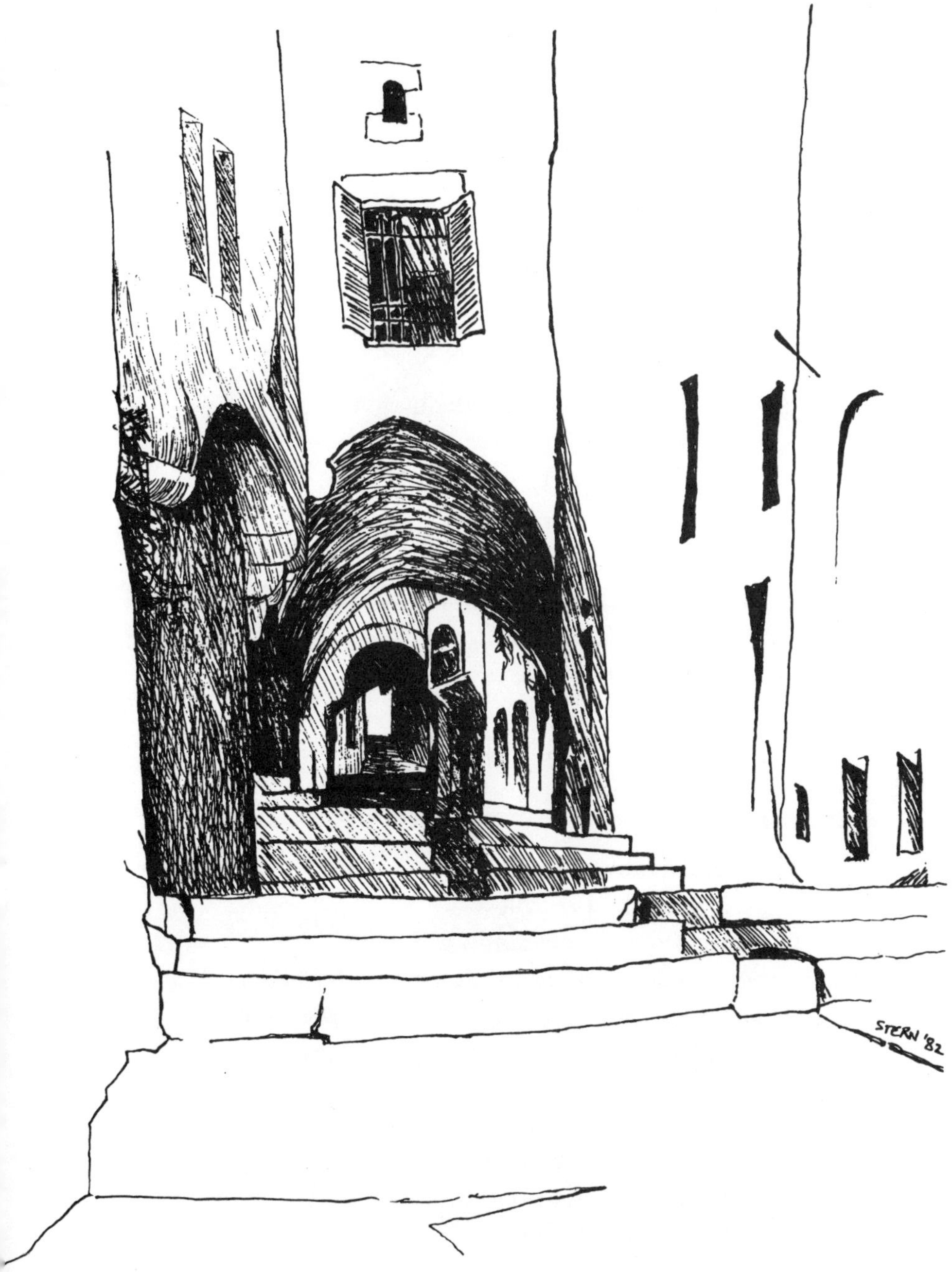
STERN '82

Cactus
by Irena Klepfisz

for my mother
Rose Perczykow Klepfisz

The pot itself was half the story.
A yellow ceramic dime store knickknack
of a featureless Mexican
with a large sombrero   pushing a wagon
filled with dirt.

The cactus was the other half.
Self-effacing   it didn't demand much
which was just as well
since she had no spare time
for delicate cultivation.
Used to just the bare essentials
it stood on our kitchen windowsill
two floors above the inhospitable soil
and neither flourished   grew
nor died.

I'd catch her eyeing it
as she stood   breathless
broiling our dinner's minute steaks
her profile centered in the windowframe.
She understood   the meaning   of both pot
and plant   still would insist there was
something extra   the colors yellow
green   or as she once explained
in her stiff   night school English:
"It is always   of importance to see
the things aesthetical."

Copyright by Irena Klepfisz.
First published in Keeper of Accounts, *Sinister Wisdom Books, 1986.*

Not Yet Visible
by Ruth Daigon

My father balances on scaffolding
high above our games.
Each time he spits a nail
and drives it in,
a wall goes up,
room dividers rise
from hopscotch squares,
a second floor
from teeter-totters,
the whole house framed on stilts.

He climbs the ladder,
waves from every window
until I catch his signal,
return it,
and find myself waving
from our top floor
at his bent frame
growing smaller
as he moves along receding avenues.

I look out
signalling my sons
who for a moment
recognize me,
signal back
then shift into a new position
straining to see something
not yet visible.

First published in Bellingham Review, *1989*.

The Seasons of the Swastika
by Henny Wenkart

the first swastika season
i was four
little biplanes flew over vienna
and from them
colored little paper swastikas
fluttered down like petals in the blossom season.

i stuffed my pockets full of blue, pink, orange thin-angled
　petals,
tried to stuff the glorious carpet of paper petals
from the sidewalk all into my pockets.

that was a sin, i could see that as soon as i got them home.
mitzi laughed, but her laugh was wrong,
and mommy shook me! screamed at mitzi!
picked me up and shook me!

The second time those petals came
I never touched one.
I was ten years old
And I never touched them.

the first swastika season
daddy held a lawyer's pass to the inner city
we could make our sunday outing to the palace garden
daddy had a pass

young soldiers in pairs let us through
to this pass only the palace itself was off limits.
still, i tantrummed for my climbing ledge along the palace wall
and serenely, his hair shining, his smile
shining,
daddy approached the sergeant: "do you
have a little child? what can i do?
she always climbs there . . ."

the first swastika season i won.

The second time they bloomed
Blood red and black
Down the buildings,
On people's arms,
High on the steeples against the sky.
I never touched them.

Safe House
by Henny Wenkart

On the tenth of November
On the day THEY call Kristallnacht
Mommy was the hero then,
Mommy was the hero.

"We are sealing off apartments,
Hurry, hurry with your packing,
You must get out, just a few things,
Hurry, we have work to do!"
And she nodded, ran down cellar,
Took the lift up to the attic,
Packed a suitcase and unpacked it,
Wrapped a compress on her throat.

In pajamas, in her wrapper,
Stalled them, stalled them with her packing,
Packed and unpacked seven hours,
"Yes, yes, yes, the baby's things,
You see sergeant, the old woman —
And my husband — should be back now —
Maid's gone off, too — such a bother —
I myself will go down cellar.
One more suitcase, that should do it,
Yes, I'll hurry, I *will* hurry."

Till the super came to say
It was over, Aktion over.
Those downstairs of us were locked out.
Those upstairs were saved by Mommy.

God, she laughed that night, eyes sparkling,
Put her clothes on, fed the women
Who had come to us for refuge
To our safe house
Saved by Mommy.

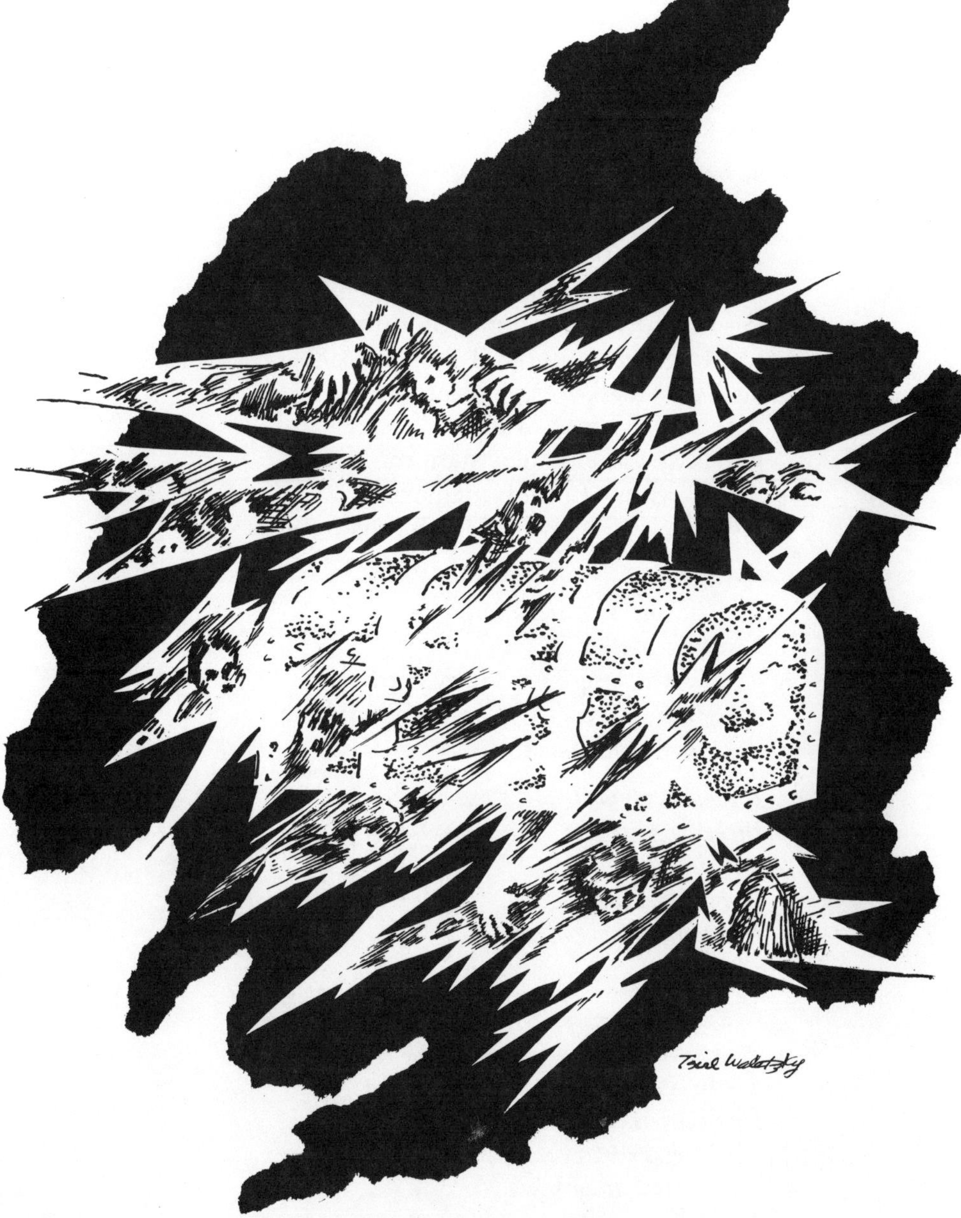

Coming Home
by Eva Reisman

I dreamed that you appeared at my side,
    Daddy, in some room
And that I heard you say my name
O the miracle of your presence!
Do I dare respond?

I grew up a borrower of alien tongues
    and alien spaces
Forever costumed in garb not my own . . .
. . .To greet you now, I must unpack
    the small dresses I outgrew
And which smell of mildew . . .
I shall sew them anew with the sparse
    threads of numb memories . . .
And they will smell of fresh mushrooms

A tranquil vision unfolds
    before my eyes today . . .
I want to tell it to you
    in the language of my birth
The one in which you called my name
    to me so sweetly

Kwiatki, szmaragdowa trawa
Blekitne niebo
Rybki plywaja
Ptaszki spiewaja
Krasnoludki na polanie

(Little flowers; the grass shines
    like emeralds
A very blue sky
Little fishes are swimming
Little birds are singing
Little red dwarves prance
    in the meadow)

You said one day that you brought me
some cake, but it turned out to be
herring . . . You tease! Remember how
angry I was at you?

Then you were taken away to a camp,
and I couldn't hide under your desk
anymore, for you to find me when you
came home . . . I saw a throng of people
carrying white bundles, marching down
the street, wailing . . . Grandma served
us alphabet soup from a can, and nobody
at the table spoke . . . It was so strange . . .

Were you very afraid at that place?

Tell me who you were
What you were thinking . . .

Do you know that you are still
    alive in me?
Do you know how empty it feels
    to say this?
Tell me that you believe
    there can be fullness!

And when you come to me again
    in a dream, Daddy
We'll say the blessing
    for the rainbow together
And the whole universe will sing

Neighborhoods
by Enid Dame

i Brighton Beach

This is the end of Brooklyn, defiant and salty.
Houses are cracking, and pavement, and people's faces.
Old men play chess on park benches. Gulls stalk the boardwalk.
In the backstreets, roses hang
scattering petals and perfume
impartially
after the rains.

The old socialists dislike the new arrivals from Russia,
who play video games and sell fish and clothes on the street.
They have come here to be capitalists.
The leftists are disappointed.
After all, they're still waiting
(in pre-war, walk-up apartments)
for Revolution to bloom.
They've kept the faith.

My mother is here on a visit. She moves on four wheels, slowly,
feeling her way down the cracked, slanting street.
She doesn't like this place:
the Russians are noisy,
the old ones are pitiful.
The Midwest, she tells me, was different
even for Jews.

Under the El,
people buy food in four languages:
sausages, marblecake, chickens, gooseberry jam, parsnip roots
knobbier than old fingers.
Here is a man with a number stitched on his arm.
The guilty Old World pays his rent
He is still sane. He raises tomatoes and roses.

He asks if we know about Hitler. He says,
"They took away, now they give."

Here is the ocean. It keeps on breathing,
sensuous, ragged. A cat on a bed,
reassuring. It has outlived
politics and religion.
It has outlived
everything
so far.

I have come here, dragging my life in a suitcase.
Once it had cracked like a New York sidewalk,
like a sea-eaten bungalow,
like the old vase my mother finds
in a second-hand shop.
"It's still good," she says. "You can use it."

This is a place of immigrants, radicals, exiles,
serious eaters and various gifts. I live here
a block from the sea and the second-hand shops. I come home
through salt-wrinkled streets
to a doorway
cluttered with roses.

First published in Confrontation, *1985.*

ii Inheritance

The tarot cards were a surprise.
I never knew my mother
to believe in revelation.
The china service for twelve
was an old acquaintance:
all those moving days
we'd wrap it gingerly —
gravyboat large as an ark, chamberpot soup tureen —
to uncrate in another new life
where she'd never use it.

Now, relatives plant trees for her in Israel,
a mythic country
she never quite believed in
before the last, disjointed year.
Till then, she claimed
no place in particular.

I carry her cat home to Brooklyn,
a city my mother distrusted.
She had no use for my ocean.
(Hers sprawls in summer photographs,
playful and blue, with a blonde beach,
promising games and renewals.

She'd stare at it for hours
as if memorizing a text.)

In Brooklyn,
the ocean's an old Jewish lady,
muttering, sloppy, with terrible manners,
dragging her cargoes of life and garbage.
She isn't pretty.   She hisses and spits.

So does my mother's cat,
tense, displaced tiger, unhappy woman.
Her mourning wails fill my house.

Will I grow used to her dissatisfaction
burning like her green eyes in the corner,
constant as a mother's?

First published in Pivot, *1985.*

iii Yahrzeit

The *yahrzeit* flame
is beating its wings in a cup
on the edge of my kitchen sink.
Its stealthy gold shadow
breathing along the wall
suddenly terrifies me:
like finding a bird in my bedroom
still alive   pulsating   nervous,
changing the shape of the day.

No intruder is ever harmless.
And, mother, I've got you cornered,
fierce memory pacing your glass cage,
houseguest with nowhere to go.
I'll lock myself in alongside you.
Today, we'll remind each other
of old connections, old journeys
from muddy, sincere Indiana
to ragged-edged Brooklyn
with all its stray cats, its ecstatic
vegetable stands.

First published in Poetry New York.

iv Untenanted

Standing over
your uninhabited body,
father,
I kept thinking,
"The building is still there."

I could picture it: the five-floor Bronx walk-up
where memory started, for you.
For fifty years, you built and rebuilt it
until it seemed real as my skin.

Leaving you,
I entered your city
on a Greyhound bus.
There, I lived quietly
among ghosts
I recognized from your stories.
Some rode the D-train all night.
Some wore fur coats in the Automat.
Some drank tea out of glasses and stared into space.
Some hung on my wall.

One wet spring
you came to see me.
I showed you the ocean at the end of my block.
We stood and watched it, a caged animal,
shrunken, grey, talking to itself.
A police car crawled down the boardwalk,
rain-battered, slow as an insect.
"The city is dying," you said.

When we found your building,
you were disappointed.
Your mother's curtains were torn down.
Nobody spoke your language.

Still, it was there,
claiming its square of the Bronx. All around
gaped holes where houses had been:
yanked up like teeth,
burnt down to their roots,
half-collapsed,
doorframes hanging, rooms exposed
like body parts in a child's instructional toy.

You said, "'This is awful. Let's go."
I thought, "At least, it's standing.
People, families, live here.
That counts for something. Doesn't it?"

We could have touched its brick sides.
They would have felt hard, yellow, ordinary.
I could have touched your hand.
We could have gone in, found your mother's door,
felt for *mezuzah* lumps under layers of paint,
tried to ask questions.

We didn't. We went back to my place,
the crooked streets, the grumbling ocean.
You said, "I shouldn't have come."

When you were dying, in another city, I was in the next room,
on the phone, arguing with a nurse.
She didn't believe what was happening.

And when I touched you
finally
you felt hard, untenanted,
yet warm,
a brick wall
still holding in the sun.

First published in Negative Capability.

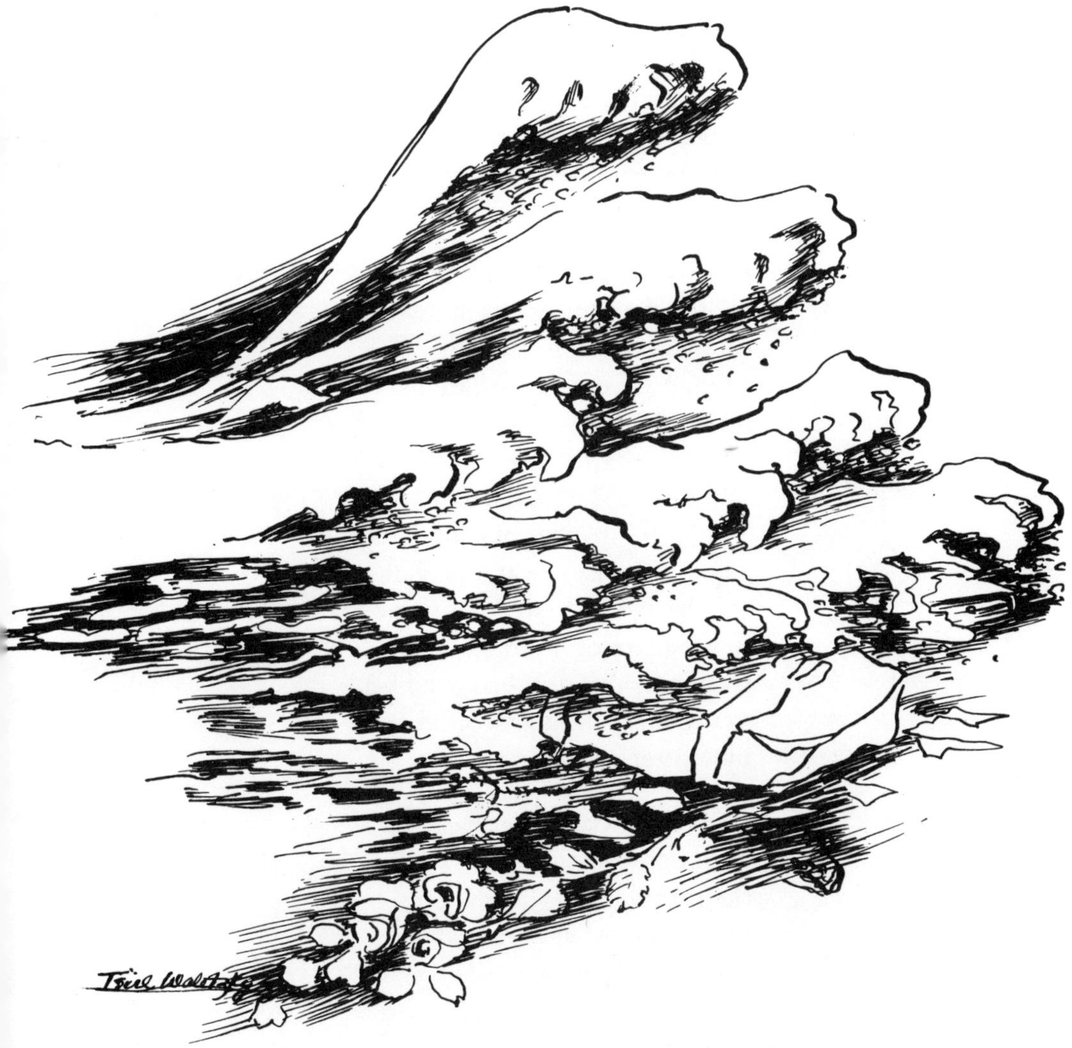

My Mother's Novel
by Marge Piercy

Married academic woman ten
years younger holding that microphone
like a bazooka, forgive
me that I do some number of things
that you fantasize but frame
impossible.   Understand:
I am my mother's daughter,
a small woman of large longings.

Energy hurled through her
confined and fierce as in a wind
tunnel.   Born to a mean
harried poverty crosshatched
by spidery fears and fitfully
lit by the explosions
of politics, she married her way
at length into the solid workingclass:
a box of house, a car she could
not drive, a TV set kept turned
to the blare of football,
terrifying power tools, used wall
to wall carpeting protected
by scatter rugs.

Out of backyard posies
permitted to fringe
the proud hanky lawn
her imagination hummed
and made honey,
occasionally exploding
in mad queen swarms.

I am her only novel.
The plot is melodramatic,
hot lovers leap out of
thickets, it makes you cry
a lot, in between the revolutionary
heroics and making good
home-cooked soup.
Understand: I am my mother's
novel daughter: I
have my duty to perform.

Published in The Moon Is Always Female, *Knopf, 1980*

On Borrowed Time
by Elizabeth Zelvin

at 76 and 80 my parents buy new tennis rackets
take up painting for the second time
and go to Israel

my mother, indefatigable voyager
traveling without a camera
has the photographer's eye
every mountain, every street is different
I swam in the Dead Sea, the Red Sea, the Med
she reports triumphantly

my parents' life is rich as the oysters
my father eats at La Coupole in Paris
visiting my sister on the way home
expatriate, exmatriate
she has been missing most of this
and envies me these years
of borrowed time

here beyond the years of anger
beyond the silences
we speak a common language
my father's jokes make me laugh again
it is again a form of grace to cry
with my head in my mother's lap

I have an intact childhood
fragile as an eggshell with the meat blown out
both parts preserved
I can still dine
in the house my parents bought
when my mother was carrying me

when I sleep in my parents' house
they make up the bed I traded in my crib for
the pine tree outside my window
still catches stars in its branches
the pine tree is still growing
it frightens me
having so much to lose

First published in I Am the Daughter, *New Rivers Press, 1981.*

Love

Tsirl Waletzky

Young Women Leave Home
by Rifka Fingerhut

When young women leave home
to find somewhere different
A mother they prefer to
The one they were becoming
They do not look back
at first
But run from the disaster
Life caving in within, revealing
deep crevices
They take roads without fresh footprints
The caves of ancient meaning
Rest in someone else's home
Somewhere else when darkness falls
The women that they turn to
see daughters without failures
The freshly travelled faces of
young spirits they once were
Other women's daughters find our mothers
quite attractive
The person that they seek out to confirm their
new directions
We grow past the disillusion in the arms of
other daughters
Young ones loving one another with the skills their
mothers taught them

California Sister
by Elizabeth Zelvin

for Anita

the thing about you and me:
we remember where we've been

yes, Anita, I know you really
have long straight hair
were gassed in People's Park
fierce and humorless, a fighter
while I was smiling for my country
against the mutter of the talking drums
a few years later I was wearing denim
dreaming utopias at home
planning next time.

now you talk computers, shake your poodle curls
California flower in your fuchsia blouse and shoes
I've sold you insurance in my blue jeans
you've played the fiddle in your tailored suit
we have lain naked in the sun together
the only nonlesbians at the pool
we are ourselves in any guise, Anita
you don't have to take your fuchsia shoes off
when you cry

remember when your brother visited
we all walked on eggshells till they cracked
and we cuddled, triple yolkmates, laughing
until bedtime, when we separated
the only way that broke no taboos
but we know love enveloped us like albumen
none of us will ever forget

as long as things keep going
voices fly faster than bombers
but when will we find time to telephone
with whom can I talk sales and revolution
who will eat ice cream in bed with me
bright green hooded bathrobe close to my purple gown
when between lie mountains, wheatfields, mountains
and cities heavy with industrial smog

write me a postcard now and then
call me when you can, remember
who you are and where you come from
some day we'll hold each other, woman friend
if the world survives

First published in I Am the Daughter, *New River Press, 1981.*

Rites de Passage
by Madeline Tiger

for Cynthia

As our bodies took shape,
to escape from dancing school
we wandered in the Reservation
to Hemlock Falls, running through stubble,
horsedung, and bottlecaps.
We took a handkerchief
between our faces,
approached each other
as we fancied lovers did,
and embraced — tight-lipped
muslin kisses,
then lay on the rocks in slips,
whispering/half afraid
of/tall intruders
and brooding about not being
asked to dance.

With my first love
I walked slowly to a clearing
among maples, near there,
worshipped
his small face, his shoulders,
his yellow hair, and refused him.

Years later
I met you
on the beach at Wildwood
with your lover/ your bosom was
spilling, your teeth
were flamboyant and
the right
of passage gleamed like dime
in your eyes.

First published in South and West, *1971.*
© *Madeline Tiger.*

My Father's Garden
by Dina Elenbogen

i

I have come back
to notice the roses
blooming in my father's garden,
the salmon ones against the fence,
the white in the center,
the red in the far corner
of the yard.

My father dreams weddings
in his yard during a spring
of his life, weddings
with white roses.
I have dreamt weddings
during my deepest sleep,
weddings without flowers

but with large pieces
of uncut fruit.

I have dreamt weddings
to the wrong man whose face
becomes unrecognizable at the altar.
I have tried the white dress on
in secret corners.

ii

Someone I love sends twigs
with small blue buds
from the Golan. I am here
to receive them, to receive
stories of his grandmother
who believed New York
was the promise.

What could she say back
to the lower east side,
the empty flower boxes
of the lower east side. Grandma,
there are no roses on the lower
east side, only tables with large
pieces of uncut fruit.

iii

My love, there are flowers
on every street corner, in vases
of limestone flats, in Jerusalem,
where you walk on the Sabbath.
When you stand alone at the wall,
it is your grandmother's hand
that touches your face.

Yesterday, before the Sabbath,
I walked the silent streets
of an American town
with someone else's son
clutching my hand.
What do the dried leaves mean
at two?

Last night, in a dream,
I carried him over puddles
as if he were my own son.
In a dream, I was
gathering white roses
from my father's garden,
bring them
to you.

April
by Henny Wenkart

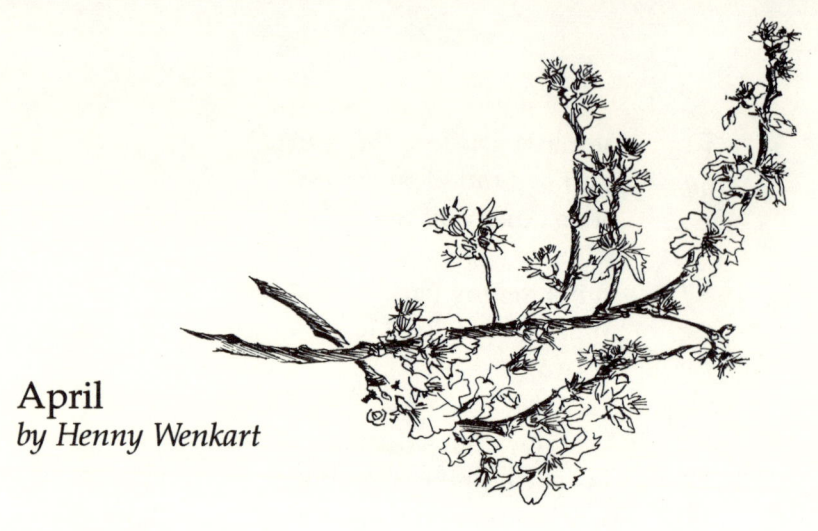

It is April

   night

      a terrace high over the Hudson.

She, seventeen
   lifts her face to a spray of blossoms under the street light,
   caught by their sweetness

   but aware

   how sweetly, also
   the curve and stretch of her slender throat give back the light.

He, twenty, gazes

                trembling

                        and catches his breath.

Desire
by S. Ben-Tov

Desire
comes like the sea wind
to the long smile of the coast;

comes in, high tide,
an ocean shuddering with weight
unbearable as glass;

we could freeze
in this clarity
piling up around the piers

that shake like sticks,
their sea-moss floating up, fanning apart
green as gems in the hard water

drowning the rocks.
The cold shocks the heart;
in a moment, you come clear;

the lover I trust
having looked out
through your eyes almost without noticing,

seen us face to face,
and come back
to my own mind.

What a waste we float in;
the taste of salt, archaic,
consuming those who drink this water down;

what a house of lives
alien to us
as the cells of our bloodstreams;

gelatinous bubble, manta wing, tentacle and shell.
The sand is full of those,
abandoned, who thought to perfect themselves;

we tread water in that peril;
desire is wide;
we cling;

back roll the pebbles
and the edgeless grains of silt,
the soft, accumulative bed

more than itself,
therefore
a promise:

tense rings of sunlight
patterning
the underwater sand

and the face of the water, passing between
the warp of the surface
and the change of depth.

The sky clears, the windows
over the bed
are blue in the morning;

the same scent rises
from both lovers lying
curled on our sides like harbors.

From During Ceasefire, *by Sharona Ben-Tov.* © *1985 by Sharona Ben-Tov. Reprinted by permission of Harper & Row Publishers, Inc.*

Patience
by Jessica Lipsky

Patience is the lesson
I am to learn.
You are the teacher.
I wait for you to come.

Effort at Speech Between Two People
by Muriel Rukeyser

Speak to me. Take my hand. What are you now?
I will tell you all. I will conceal nothing.
When I was three, a little child read a story about a rabbit
who died, in the story, and I crawled under a chair:
a pink rabbit: it was my birthday, and a candle
burnt a sore spot on my finger, and I was told to be happy

Oh, grow to know me. I am not happy.
    I will be open:
Now I am thinking of white sails
    against a sky like music,
like glad horns blowing, and birds tilting,
    and an arm about me.
There was one I loved, who wanted to live, sailing.

Speak to me. Take my hand. What are you now?
When I was nine, I was fruitily sentimental,
fluid: and my widowed aunt played Chopin,
and I bent my head on the painted woodwork,
    and wept.

I want now to be close to you. I would
link the minutes of my days close,
   somehow, to your days.

I have liked lamps in evening corners,
   and quiet poems.
There has been fear in my life.
     Sometimes I speculate
On what a tragedy his life was, really.

Take my hand. Fist my mind in your hand.
    What are you now?
When I was fourteen, I had dreams of suicide,
And I stood at a steep window, at sunset,
   hoping toward death:
if the light had not melted clouds and
   plains to beauty,
if light had not transformed that day,
   I would have leapt.
I am unhappy. I am lonely. Speak to me.

I will be open. I think he never loved me:
he loved the bright beaches, the little lips of foam
that ride small waves, he loved the veer of gulls:
he said with a gay mouth: I love you.
   Grow to know me.

What are you now? If we could touch one another,
if these our separate entities could come to grips,
clenched like a Chinese puzzle . . . yesterday
I stood in a crowded street that was live with people,
and no one spoke a word, and the morning shone.
Everyone silent, moving . . . Take my hand.
   Speak to me.

1935, United States.

Predestination
or, Love is Not Enough
by Florence B. Freedman

I kissed the frog firmly . . .
He shrank within himself,
Then leaped mightily from my enfolding hands —
Fiercely resisting princehood.

zip-door johnny
by Marion D. S. Dreyfus

he'd stand out in the
hall, a
   sweet knowing
part-smile on his
   toughguy
   vulnerable face
with his bomber
jacket all
done up — except
his zipper
   down,
   his member doing a
   shy slow-take
   outside the
   iron babyteeth
wondering abashedly
   what in hell am I
   doing out here?

and whether he did it
for shock
   or giggle
each time I opened
my door
   to him
the hot suffused softy
making its
popular appearance
out in the
scandal zone
   (#'s 1914 and 1916
   plus the left-hand
   side of the hall), I'd
laugh and collapse
a present! my goodie!
fall into high octane
   major-league lust
   we recognised under-
   neath as love
and invite him inside
   deep inside
bringing him onto my
side for
a year and some,
out & in for four more
the ziptrick never
failing to
   quash
   disapproval of
his sometimes
pissass
ways

Secrets of the Therapeutic Relationship
by Elizabeth Zelvin

the pale eyes flashing in his dark face
the slash of cheekbone and brow
pierce me with secret pleasure
he is arresting in his pride and anger
his beauty that of pose
of a stillness like a dancer's
but look again, he is rigid with fear, untrusting
as some lithe animal frozen in the tall grass

between therapist and client
more tender intimacies are shared
than if we two lay touching on a bed

the woman he loved got cancer, he speaks of that
she would not let him see her shrunk into her bones
he whose looks invite the robust flesh of strangers
she could not imagine how endearing
he found her wizened as a baby
her hair just fuzzing in after the chemo
instead, she slipped away from him in coma
he never got to say goodbye

he gets mugged on the subway
he brings me his humiliation
deflated, he looks pitifully smaller
after being kicked in head and groin
called *pretty boy* as he lay helpless
and left, contemptuously, with unscarred face

I listen as he stammers, fumbling
among memories, unspent mourning and fresh outrage
full of pain and hope and future
at the end he takes my hands, so moving in his need
that I remember, for the first time in many days
why I felt called to do this work I do

his mother finds him, two weeks later, in the morning
still as the effigy of an entombed knight
his battle over   cold as stone

later, at a staff party
I cast aside my workday guise, austere, sedate
to dance with such abandon
that they believe I have revealed myself at last
so sinuous in amethyst and black velvet
that I surprise them all
the doctors pompous and glassy as stuffed owls
the secretaries with their powdered breasts
they do not know that I am grieving

they do not know I loved you

The Yosom
by Blu Greenberg

Yeshiva handsome:
A hooked nose
Gray, gray eyes
Rosy cheeks
Over good bones.

Curly brown hair
Under a hat
Tilted slightly back
The perfect chic of a modern yeshiva bocher.

He knew how to get around
How to "hondle"
Sniff opportunity
He was kind, funny, clever
Though at times moody
At times a bit distant
We knew he had been saved by miracles.

He loved Sarah
The oldest of five daughters
Of a great, booming family.
"No!" said her father
A charitable man,
"A yosom
Raised by rebbes. . ."
"No," said her mother
A woman of good works,
"Without a father
How will he
Know to be one?"
"Better to wait," said Tante Esther
"Find another," said the wise old bobba.
"No. . ." said my friend
To her Beloved.

The grey eyes darkened
The yosom
Straightened his hat.

Antonio's Night
by Lynn Saul

I whisper
"*yo soy marrano*"
because I think
I recognize you.

You remember the word
from your history books,
secret Jews of the Spanish
Inquisition, but you didn't know

some had come to America.
There's not much
I need to explain.

> *In the illustration*
> *Don Carvajal's sister Isabel*
> *stands barebreasted*
>
> *before the table of*
> *Inquisitors. She is so young*
> *in her boyish undershorts,*
> *but her firm, full breasts*
>
> *refuse to be embarrassed. Later*
> *they will stand her on a cord of wood,*
> *she will whisper "Shema" over the flames.*

All night, we slap mosquitos
from each other's backs. When I whisper
"*te quiero*," you hear
"*soy marrano*," so we make love

as though we've known each other
four hundred years. If I did not tell you
who we are, this would be another
one-night stand. But we have recognized

each other. *Nuestro gente.* Before dawn
I'll wish that I could make you pregnant,
make you give me a daughter
who could teach me how to kindle *Shabbat*

back in New Mexico,
where I pick peaches
and raise pigs.

old softie
by Marion D.S. Dreyfus

he talks so thick
before bed
during
      not after, when
      he goes, spent
      to keen
      his unspurt seed
it almost makes
me forget how a
hard cock
would be so much
more talkative

his tough spate
so full of
jismy ideas

        afoam with lust
        I ride in
        tourny waves
        so far alone
   midwife to crispy
   postun-
   coital dark;
   this stark adonis
   bobbing unpedestalled

A Confession
by Judith Heineman

I have gone to the genealogy room
of The New York Public Library
— Room 315 —
and looked up the death records
for the past five years
expecting to find
your name
After all these years
I'm still looking for you
I want to go back to
sixteen
when everything was new and fresh
and you . . .

I was sure you were dead
judging from how you lived
but I couldn't find your name
Maybe you died somewhere else
or you're alive . . .
But not in Brooklyn

Your brother's name is listed in the book
returned from Manhattan I see
and so is your father's
And a woman with your last name
Your wife?
Your sister?
Where is your name?

How electric blue-
white
the space between us was that one evening
Memory is more present
than reality
That time years ago
is alive to me still
I want to find
me
all over again
at the beginning
Not that I would do
anything differently . . .

In Lieu of Letters
by Sharon Cameron

Two days a week I teach. I try
To show them differences: we fumble on
Sometimes I feel the need to write to you;
I fight it with the stern insistent pride
It takes to silence students when they're wrong —
I only sanction certain kinds of speech.

A month has passed. I do not write or speak
Your name. No more to watch the tall men
Winding their way home. Or to single out
A step in the half light of evening
Or startle at the shadows that lengthen by my side.

Living in Sin
by Adrienne Rich

She had thought the studio would keep itself;
no dust upon the furniture of love.
Half heresy, to wish the taps less vocal,
the panes relieved of grime. A plate of pears,
a piano with a Persian shawl, a cat
stalking the picturesque amusing mouse
had risen at his urging.
Not that at five each separate stair would writhe
under the milkman's tramp; that morning light
so coldly would delineate the scraps
of last night's cheese and three sepulchral bottles;
that on the kitchen shelf among the saucers
a pair of beetle-eyes would fix her own —
envoy from some black village in the mouldings . . .
Meanwhile, he, with a yawn,
sounded a dozen notes upon the keyboard,
declared it out of tune, shrugged at the mirror,
rubbed at his beard, went out for cigarettes;
while she, jeered by the minor demons,
pulled back the sheets and made the bed and found
a towel to dust the table-top,
and let the coffee-pot boil over on the stove.
By evening she was back in love again,
though not so wholly but throughout the night
she woke sometimes to feel the daylight coming
like a relentless milkman up the stairs.

"Living in Sin" is reprinted from THE FACT OF A DOORFRAME, Poems Selected and New, 1950–1984, *by Adrienne Rich, with the permission of the author and W. W. Norton & Company, Inc. Copyright © 1984 by Adrienne Rich. Copyright © 1975, 1978 by W. W. Norton & Company, Inc. Copyright © 1981 by Adrienne Rich.*

Words for a Song
by Helen Neville

I do not mind
that he touches you, speaks to you, tells you everything,
or that I call him in vain.
What is abominable is that he
has become another country —
so much resembling the one I knew
in every outward view
as to tempt me to walk through it over and over again;
finding there breath like a noose, a hand
sharper than knives, words spoken
in a language I cannot hope to understand,
and all the beautiful marble columns broken.

1959, United States.

Harey At

Brynna Bloomfield

Mazel Tov!
by Merle Feld

Once
I was at a wedding
and I told the bandleader,
"When the bride and groom come in,
play something really *frailach*,
because we all want to dance and lift them on chairs."

But the caterer came over, and she said,
"We're on a tight schedule here:
smorgasbord
roast beef
Viennese table
and another wedding at six.
We don't have time for dancing till after the soup."

I looked at her.
I looked at the bandleader.
My eyes narrowed, and I said,
"We'll all be dancing when the bride and groom come in
and we'll lift them on chairs.
You can play along with us, or we'll sing for ourselves."

So we did.
And he did.
And screw the caterer.

Cutting the Jewish Bride's Hair
by Ruth Whitman

It's to possess more than the skin
that those old world Jews
exacted the hair of their brides.

Good husband, lover of the Torah,
does the calligraphy of your bride's hair
interrupt your page?

Before the clownish friction of flesh
creating out of nothing
a mockup of its begetters,
a miraculous puppet of God,
you must first divorce her from her vanity.

She will snip off her pride,
cut back her appetite to be devoured,
she will keep herself well braided,
her love's furniture will not endanger you,
   but this little amputation
   will shift the balance of the universe.

First Published in The Marriage Wig and Other Poems, *Harcourt, Brace Jovanovitch, 1968.*

Why I Understand World Literature
by Shulamith Surnamer

*"And thou shalt not approach a menstruant
woman to uncover her nakedness." Leviticus 18:19*

1.

nipple-length
tresses
auburn-dyed

cascading falls

reflect me back
in the mirrored bathroom
at the Mikvah
this Sabbath Eve

2.

across the continental divide
I feel you
My Angelic Satan

I feel you

telepathically invading

invading
this holy chamber

with your midnight
ruminations
of me
when you are not
HE
for whom I now prepare
when you are not
the Bridegroom
for whom I immerse myself
in these real waters
and not some phantasea

3.

near to me

the resident male

ever nearer to me

the First Man

moving near to me
still nearer to me

sensuously short-circuits
the remote wizardry
of the long-distance broadcaster
with his skillful husbandry

near to me
very, very near to me

4.

elsewhere in the night
your sister/wife

the missing one

lodged in that idyllic resort
the paradise still unchartered

Lilith, the long sleeping, stirs

howls as she readies
for earth-wide winged flight
howls as she conceives
what is to be

  howls the Ineffable   howls

5.

and they say

only GOD

Great Author of All

knows the full text
twists and turns
plot past-old
now-new, future-next
from the singular dreidle
he/she does spin
the one lettered

Adam   *Aleph*
Lilith   *Lamed*
Chava   *Chet*
Satan   *Sin*
he/she does spin

© 1984, 1988 by Shulamith Surnamer.

Meditation on Aleph
by Lucy Cohen Schmeidler

Why do you say my sound is "ah?"
In a phonetic alphabet,
each letter has its sound, but I have none.
Say then my sound is silence? More than silence,
mine is the sound of listening, yearning, reaching
for my companion vowel.

Bedecken
by Henny Wenkart

Whose smile is that?
Seated amid her women —
    her attendants in light and darker blues,
    her mother, his mother,
My daughter beams at her beloved
    (the violin is singing, "A woman of valor who can find?")
Where he comes followed by his father, her father,
    her brothers, his brothers.
But whose smile is that on her face?

It is the smile of their private hours.
He is not surprised by it.

It transforms her face
Into not her face as I know her.
    A little it is like the smile of my mother,
    But not very like that.
It is
My daughter's smile as she is the woman of her man,
Properly unknown to me.

He puts the veil down over her face.

First published in Response, *1988.*

Elegy
by Madeline Tiger

for Eva Hesse 1936 - 1970

We were bridesmaids in the same wedding
younger than the city   then
our nipples   our toes   pointed
we bought white shoes
at Chandler's   you resisted
expense   you   felt   awkward
in the rose-bud dress
your beauty was converting
          into dreamy molds
poses beyond your body
and, pulling back   your black   hair,
you seemed to be making love
somewhere else
while we performed earthy rituals
for a friend.

On the bus
from Bergdorf's
you entered
desperate questions
about love and you took me
to the loft
where the Irishman was
sculpting
waiting to embrace you.

At the Plaza the band was playing
"Never on Sunday"
you barely danced   I wondered
if you had felt the minutes
as we flooded ahead of Cynthia
Tom wore a winter suit
to the wedding   he danced

wildly said fuck
the waiter
grabbed you around
the pink rosebuds fitted
at your waist bridesmaid!
You both wanted
he wanted to go home.

With your lonely hands
you compressed all wedding
and lived holy — Eva —
through a new ritual you went on
marrying marrying

First published in The Little Magazine, *1972.*

Once More With You
by Helen Papell

These days of love are lollipops
dropped free to a child

a woman's shoulder-flutter
Is sister
to a crane's wing in a field of corn,
The crane hovers over its mate startled with moon

I know that love is witch's brew and
witches were the ones who burned,

And my ancestor Ruth who rounded
her apron with grains
comes to warn me of her fate:
fill the eyes of a he
and you will grandmother a king.

I'm not a child; and though I hear
years hungry as jaws
stalk behind the coupling and the corn,

I'm once more with you
wind-stunned.

The first time we made Shabbos together
by Merle Feld

The first time we made Shabbos together
in our own home
(it wasn't really "our home"
it was your third floor walk-up
and we weren't even engaged yet)
I had cooked chicken
my first chicken
with a whole bulb of garlic
(my mother never used garlic)
and we sat down at that second-hand chrome table
in the kitchen.
It was all so ugly that we turned out the lights.
Only the Shabbos candles flickered.

And then you made kiddush.

I sat there and wept—
Oh God, you have been so good to me!
Finally, for the first time in my life,
you gave me something I wanted.
This man, whose soul is the soul of Ein Gedi.
We will be silent together
We will open our flowers in each other's presence.

And indeed we have bloomed through the years.

You Sowed in Me, Not a Child
by Celia Dropkin

You sowed in me, not a child
but yourself.
So it's you growing in me daily,
greater and more distinct.
There's no room left inside me
for myself
and my soul lies like a dog at your feet
growing fainter and fainter.
But, dying into you,
I still, even now, can make you songs.

Russia and U.S. 1917.
Translated from Yiddish by Adrienne Rich.

First published in A Treasury of Yiddish Poetry *ed. Howe and Greenberg, Holt, Rinehart and Winston, 1969.*

Housewife
by Susan Fromberg Schaeffer

What can be wrong
That some days I hug this house
Around me like a shawl, and feel
Each window like a tatter in its skin,
Or worse, bright eyes I must not look through?

Now my husband stands above me
As high as ever my father did,
And I am in that house of dolls which
When young I could not shrink to.

I feel the shrinkage in each bone.
No matter what I do, my two girls
Spoil like fruit. Already they push us back
Like too-full plates. They play with us
Like dolls.

The road before the house is like a wish
That stretches out and out and will not
Stop, and the smallest hills are built
Like steps to the slippery moon,
But I
Circle this lit house like any moth
And see the day open its fingers
To disclose the stone — which hand?
Which hand? and the stone in both.

Once, I drove my car into a tree.
The bottles in the back
Burst like tubular glass beasts,
Giving up the ghost. My husband
Thought it was the road. It was.

In the rear-view mirror, it curved and curled,
Longer and stronger than the road ahead,
A question of perspective, I thought then.
I watched it till it turned, and I did not.
I breathed in pain like air,
As if I, the rib, had cracked.

I did not feel this pain, not then,
Almost in my mouth. I wiggle this life
And find it loose. Like my girls,
I would pull it out, would watch
Something new and white
Push like mushrooms from the rich red soil.
But there is just this hole, this bone.

So I live inside my wedding ring,
Inside its arch,
Multiplying the tables of my days,
Rehearsing the lessons of this dish, that sleeve,
Wanting the book that no one wrote,
Loving my husband, my children, my home,
Wanting to go.

Do others feel like this? Where do they go?

Continuing
by Madeline Tiger

each one had defenses, they said
the sheets were full of static
sometimes, when they went to bed
he biting drunk, she swollen
with silences
they pulled the blankets to shreds
and wrapped themselves separate as
shrouds

in the museum sand held skeletons
nothing could pry the fingers
from the clench,
and the round spine reminded them
all humans
are alone   in time
they must uncurl, combine, beg
and forgive one another
it is nearly impossible
to live under one roof without speech
or that slow growing into
something   they needed
to name love, for want of another way
to say how lonely it is here
on earth
and how the nights are cold

First published in We Become New, *Bantam, 1975.* © *Madeline Tiger*

The Enemy is the Dark
by Phyllis Koestenbaum

The enemy is the dark
and I am my own gentle defender; I aim my bow
towards the bend in the night beyond, the past
which waits for me like a trap
as I descend delicately without purpose winding stairs, seashore
cabins I have never seen and mountain ones where I peed
into an old pot after thunderstorms.

I expect to be revisited in my quiet double bed
with its orange flowered sheets and its smell of loss
and gain. Each fall to where I've been is a lonely careful climb:
I don't forget.

I had thought I was abused but when I woke at night
dry in my throat and dry in my heart
he gave me cool water in a yahrzeit glass.

First published in That Nakedness, *1982,* © *Phyllis Koestenbaum.*

Sunday
by Marcia G. Rosen

Alone on Sunday,
I envy you
with your families, with
tables set,
newspapers on the floor,

children waiting,
husbands.
I envy the intimacy,
the sharing,
talking,
planning,
family afternoons,
together.
Then I remember,
the whistle of suburban trains
flashing to the city,
children with friends,
a face silent
in front of the television,
laundry tumbling,
something for me to do
because I felt so lonely
with you.

A Woman of Valor, Who Can Find?
by Renee Alfandary

Once upon a time in Concord, California, there lived a woman
   of valor with
her husband and two children
and her worth was far above rubies,
although she did not possess rubies
only a diamond pin from Davidson and Licht's
and a strand of pearls from her aunt Rebecca
and a turquoise bracelet from her mother-in-law
who did not think much of this son's wife
because our woman of valor did not seek wool and flax
and work willingly with her hands
as a good woman of valor should.

This woman of valor did not consider a field and buy it.
She considered the dresses at I. Magnin and charged them.
And her hands did not hold her spindle.
They held the wheel of her Safari station wagon
on her way to luncheon with the girls,
and her creative writing class
and her tennis class
and the Geary Theatre which was playing "A Doll's House" by Ibsen
(that's about a woman of valor gone wrong.)
The heart of her husband did safely trust in her
and he had no lack of gain
because the woman of valor had joined Hadassah
and ORT and Sisterhood and B'nai Brith and Brandeis.
And she did stretch her hands out to the poor
whenever her WASP neighbor rang her doorbell to ask for a
  donation.
Yea, she did reach forth her hand to the needy,
because that neighbor *always* mentioned
that her own father was prejudiced against Catholics,
and Blacks, and Mexicans, and Others
but that SHE was not like that
(you know, prejudiced against Others).
Our woman of valor
looked well to the ways of her household
and ate not the bread of idleness.
But every Sabbath, her children rose and said:
"Mom, I have to go now, 'bye."
And her husband also
and he did not praise her,
although she did him good and not evil
all the days of her life.
A man of valor, who can find?

First published in The Reconstructionist, *1975.*

Housing Shortage
by Naomi Replansky

I tried to live small.
I took a narrow bed.
I held my elbows to my sides.
I tried to step carefully
And to think softly
And to breathe shallowly
In my portion of air
And to disturb no one.

Yet see how I spread out and I cannot help it.
I take myself more and more, and I take nothing
That I do not need, but my needs grow like weeds,
All over and invading; I clutter this place
With all the apparatus of living.
You stumble over it daily.

And then my lungs take their fill.
and then you gasp for air.

Excuse me for living,
But, since I am living,
Given inches, I take yards,
Taking yards, dream of miles,
And a landscape, unbounded
And vast in abandon.

And you dreaming the same.

First published in Ring Song, *Scribner, 1952.*

The Contract
by Sherry Reiter

He lay on the hospital bed
    still as marble
    his grey spirit hovering
    unsure of its direction
— Please, Lord, don't take him
    He's too sweet to be taken
    it would be so unfair
— But Sherry,
    I have to take him, you know that
— Not now, I whispered
    He's too young
    I'm too young
    The children are too young
    Don't do it
He did not move
Strong curve of jaw
    eyelash to cheek—
Silence.
— I'll make a deal with you
I'll be good. I'll be better
Better than I've ever been
I won't complain
I'll do the laundry
Clean the house
Make sure the rice is not overdone
Just don't take him now

— I've got to take him sometime
— Give me a few more years, please
Just a few more years
The silence quivered — broken by living breath
— Don't do this, I beg you
for the children's sake

for my sake —
Oh, I'm being selfish again —
For his sake, please
— I must tell you, I'll take him
when you least expect it. Prepare yourself.
The eyelashes fluttered
Green-blue eyes met mine, confused
— Are you here? Where am I?
— You're with me, I replied.

My Jewish Life Line
by Peninnah Schram

My Jewish life scribbled
across a page
ink swept across a white
paper — and —
suddenly my Jewish life in front
of me —
I left out the parts that would
make me cry
and chose to write in the
simchas —
My whole life as a cantor's child
reflected that life
How well I remember polishing
the silver collar for his big
enveloping talit —
(But then we called it his talis.)
Sitting in the Suka wearing our
winter coats
and singing duets at the
Chanuka concerts.
But there was no one year or date
that I could write on that line
for this.
And though I put down my
wedding date
Which was the beginning of
my Jewish home
I could not mark down that my
widow's home lost the
Jewish family feeling
And I was alone — only a
mother —

no longer a Jewish wife.
A line stays on the paper
— But my life and line continue —

Widow
by Florence B. Freedman

i

Death is not a striding reaper
Wielding a scythe.

He is a shabby whittler
Who leans over your bed each night,
Pen-knife in hand,
Furtively paring the flesh between skin and bones,
Disclosing the skull structure,
Hollowing the eye sockets.
Articulating the joints of fingers and toes.

Tonight he is carving delicate eyelids
to place upon your eyes
When their light is gone.

ii

I heard Death's rattled warning
Before he plunged his venomed tongue
Into your heart.

iii

I can't remember the weather
The day you died.
That is, I don't remember
How it was outside.

iv

From being a full half
I became a diminished whole.
We became *I*.
They became *she*.
A generous *ours* became a meagre *mine*.

Better to have died and been born again . . .

Perhaps the first has happened.

v

There was a reservoir of tears
   in other years.
Tonight the dam is high.

There was a spate of tears
   in other years.
Tonight the stream is dry.

There was a storm of tears
    in other years.
Tonight — a cloudless sky.

Break, dam!
Flow, stream!

Burst cloud,
Tonight!

Or I will die.

vi

"Dear Feelings," I wrote,
"I haven't heard from you in a long time.
"We used to be so close
"I thought you were part of me.
"Now tears fill my eyes
"Only when dust particles lodge there,
"And my embraces are remembered gestures."

I ended the postcard,
"Dear Feelings, wish you were here."

vii

You came in a dream last night.
I shivered till light.
At dawn I said
The dead should stay dead.

But in my garden where you stepped
From frozen earth a crocus leapt,
Its tongue of flame
Sounding your name.

Come tonight.
I'll feel no fright,
But welcome my homeless dead
To my lonely bed.

viii

"How did you get to be a rock?"
The young widow asked.

"I started as a pebble,"
I replied.
"Time passed and I became a small stone,
"Then a larger stone,
"And, finally, a rock.
"You will be a rock, too, in time."

"But I'm not even a pebble," she murmured.
"I'm just a grain of sand."

ix

A bit of iron for my spine;
A visor for my chin,
A leash to keep my fears in line,
An extra layer of skin —

Now let my day begin!

Di Kinder

Tsirl Waletzky

Her Eyes Tell Me
by Helen Papell

Pigeons see me as a five foot five
slice of bread,
My tenth floor terrace in a skyscraper
is a birth hut.

I don't want to share. Move
to canyon country, I tell the vagrant
nesting on my cement. I'll be happy
to visit pigeons in binoculars.
Go where seeds are not covered by a can
of sidewalk to peel,
Go where only eagles threaten.
Here the wind in my vacuum cleaner
has claws.

I hear a policeman shout. Below,
a woman has built a hut of cardboard slices,
a child sleeps on warm air
blown through a cellar grill.
Her eyes tell me a mother must nest
on any rock.

First published in Gryphon, *1988.*

Shopping Advice
by Henny Wenkart

Fresh is much better than frozen.
You'll hear that frozen is more predictable
   and controlled
But take my advice, fresh is the way to go.
They are talking this evening
   not about vegetables to feed their children
But sperm

To make them.

O yes, they want it all, but with a difference —
They are game to make it themselves.
If they must,
Alone.

Maybe it is more the same than different
Maybe it was never really about shopping, but about company
Women give that to one another
   whatever they are forced to be doing.

Here are Jewish women unwilling to die childless.
"May you see your children's children," says the blessing.

But their questions!
What will be my child's position halachically?
My child's options?
(Subtext: will prospective inlaws reject?)

How to tell her — the fickleness of Jewish inlaws . . .
   Accepting . . . rejecting . . .

The questions!
Raising a child alone, how will it be each time a sitter takes over?

How tell her — two generations of women have raised their
   child alone.
   Why else did they need, out in those suburbs,
   their daily koffee klatch fixes,
   their shopping advice?

Why am I here? Past menopause and my three golden ones in
   my quiver —
I know for certain: It is not as voyeuse.

I have the right.

A Mother's Tisha B'Av, July 1984
by Annette Bialik Harchik

Bitter is the word
for love that
I would name.
Bitter. To love
so hard
bowels burn,
heart churns
in a caldron of pain,
tongue scorched speechless.
Love. Bitterlove.
To want and
hope so deeply.
To have grown to make room
for another
only to discharge
my child
my missed-child
missing.

Prayer on the Approach of Accouchement
by Fanny Neuda

The tehinot or personal prayers for women written by Fanny Neuda touched every facet of women's lives in the nineteenth century. Her poignant prayers, such as those for a child moving to a foreign land or for a husband who is traveling far from home, reveal the uncertainties and fears that were a part of a woman's existence.

Oh, my God! Soon, soon approaches the great hour
when I shall give birth to another being,
According to Thy wise ordination. O God!

Thou knowest my weakness, Thou wilt pardon me
That I look toward that hour with dread and anxiety.
For Thou, Omniscient One, alone knowest
What that hour shall be unto me.

Therefore I call unto Thee, from the depths of my soul.
Fortify me with strength and courage in the hour of danger,
God of Mercy! Grant that the life of my child may not
    be my death!
Shorten the woes and pains that await me,
Let Thy help be nigh unto me in the moment of danger,
And do not remember the multitude of my sins.
Convert, O God! my pain into delight
At the lovely sight of a living, well-formed and healthy
    babe,
Whose heart may ever be dedicated unto Thee.
Lord! Have mercy upon me!
Into Thy hand I confide my life,
Keep and preserve me from all evil.
        Amen.

Vienna, 1878.
Translated from the German by M. Mayer.
Translation first published in Hours of Devotion, *L.H. Frank, 1878.*

So Open We Conceive
by Chana Bell

for Elana

i

She said   you'll find what you need here
So we eat the mushrooms
the heads   the stems   the roots
I sit in the earth

become the green of grass growing
know I am rich soil for a child

I push away the diaphragm
no dam to block life's force

ii

My middle a ripe melon
Dreams of blood rites
I swim in unison
with the being within me swimming
muscles ripple in pure animal joy
We call you Simcha — celebration

iii

Contractions   mountainous waves
one upon the other   hour upon hour
Some I ride   others carry me
I am getting so tired
I pick up the jagged granite rock
carved in the Negev
by God's harsh breath
I explore each rough edge
touching raw desert power
that is the Sabra in me
the strength
that can labor through a day
and a night
and yet another day

iv

Push Phil says
I push for two hours
with my belly and thighs
with my eyes and cheeks
till I see black hair
then a head
till cut open   one last push
Elana slips out in a rush of blood

Oh Elana   how long I have waited
through thirty-four hours of labor
through nine months of pregnancy
through thirty years of wanting to build roots
My parents gave birth to their hope
resurrecting life out of ashes
I give birth to you   little tree

© *1980 by Chana Bell.*

The Field Anthropologist Gives Birth
by S. Ben-Tov

I hate the Mundugumor
who won't give a crying infant the breast; look,
they are hanging the babies in baskets. How they come
marching, tribes ribboned and tufted, striding uneven as shadows
under swampwater moons, over cloudgrass savannah, advancing

gourd leg, spear leg, drum- and bowl-bellied, their raised
arms, sun-poured metal, their eyes
pale slivers of reed! They are bringing
flocks of hands circling
and feet to stampede.

I could squat on a hillside,
a steep slope plumed with trees; too late.
She is sheathed in me as I am:
a husk that gapes, giving
the lesson past artifacts
wrought, sewn, hammered, thought, inscribed, memorized; all
sweep back as she advances, naked and strong to the pass.
I can follow this pain with my mind,
follow the discipline driving her out.
My pelvis is scored with electric needles, the cut separates
into a band of light, a rift opens, a gulch
of light! A knife rings between the lips
of the Balinese girl whose closed eyes see, her soles
of a tranced dancer pummel the ground, she palms the haft,
smiles, and the faces flock round like applause, grins
crack wide like canoes nudging and tipping me
into the rocktoothed cataract, bushels of water
kick down my spine, the lines snap free!

Coils unravel and the swift water fades.
Her dawn head, bloodfeathered. My child,
your serious face.

From During Ceasefire, *by Sharona Ben-Tov © 1985 by Sharona Ben-Tov, Reprinted by permission of Harper & Row Publishers, Inc.*

My Friends Baked Cake and We Ordered Lox and Whitefish from the Deli
by Merle Feld

I stood there shoulder to shoulder with the men
when they hacked a piece off your little thing—
could I really sit in the room next door
and let my fantasies run wild when I heard you cry?

And yet, at the crucial moment, I wasn't watching.
I was staring off into space at some invisible focal point.
The same one I'd stared at through the hours of labor?
Maybe.
Maybe the same one Sarah stared at
when Abraham took her baby up to the mountain.

I'm not angry, but you know,
you're a little weird, you male Jewish God.
What do you need with all those foreskins anyway?

Babies
by Madeline Tiger

Nowadays they wear
these babies hung
in pouches, little
canvass slingseats they
strap on their fronts

Fathers & mothers
sport their infants out
one at a time, one to a pair,

carefully conceived (it seems)
and borne everywhere out there

When I was young
my babies were boom boom
boom boom boom, I carried them
hard: first, of course,
on my groin, heavy melons,
and then in my arms or
on my hips, often
two at a time, one on my hand,
one at my breast,
one holding my skirt or getting
its arm wrapped somehow around my leg,

always in a rush and a crush
and a chaos of sweaters, buntings,
blankets, hoods, all disarrayed, all
rosy and alarming and careless, happily
wearing me out

These placid workers
seem to take their babies in stride,
the little ones fit
in the compact sacks
and stay still — even in shops,
meetings, concerts, museums, all day outdoors, even
trekking up mountains

> *I saw one on the front of a lovely
young blond mother, on Blue Mountain in the slippery fall
debris that covered the steep rocks, and she had another
trailing after, or climbing before her, and at the top,
among the multitudes of tourists and all the foliage
turning red/yellow/gold/glorious, she sat right down,
opened the carrier sling, opened her blouse, turned
into her own circle and had him nursing; then, soon,
they were packed and strapped to go back down, husband
rounding things up, getting shoes tied, getting in
formation, hup hup, and she blithely clamboring down,
just like that*

wherever the busy parent is inclined
to include the family bundle

Ruth Paradise

Mine
are gone — off in their cities and banks and classes and
airplanes and labs and cars and canyons and love affairs,
off in their houses and couches and recipes and programs
and far away languages of marriage.

I hardly ever see them in front of me,
but it seems the more compact they get
in the sacks of life they sling themselves
into, the more, as before, they won't
hold still: They burst out of
the bindings, they flail and call
and cry and tickle me, they
whisper their strange unpredictable
messages, draping their legs
and running their fingers,
bobbing their heads and
singing their funny little sad songs, all
heavily heavily, never in front
where I can keep track
and make them stay put; always
all over the back of my mind.

7. Heartbeat
by Henny Wenkart

All that long time
While my little girl
Carried you inside her
My name for you was HB
For heartbeat.

That was all that they could see
On that first sonogram
Of you.

O my Heartbeat,
My Danny
Why did I think I would be
Like everybody else
When I never was before?
But they said,
They all kept saying
Wait! There's no thrill like it!
Just to see your little grandchild
In the hospital under glass.

Then the whole long day
While you and she
Labored to get disentangled
I arranged *her* baby pictures
In an album
And I cried,
Waited,
Felt your head bashing against bone, Danny,
Heartbeat,
Felt your ears crumple.

It was Shabbes and your uncles at the table
While we waited
Made a special brochah for the firstborn in Israel
And another for those in pain.

Next morning there she was
My little girl
Battered, worn out, pale — and they asked me
Have you seen him?
Have you looked?

But I had come to see MY baby.

First SHE had to heal.
First I had to see her nurse you
And become your world,
See you thirsting for her with your eyes.

A double-edged joy, that, to be sure,
And peculiarly
Secondhand.

Furthermore it isn't true, the other nonsense
They all told me.
You don't worry less.
The worry over someone so tiny
And so helpless
Is poignantly compounded by the worry's secondhandness.
Not I, but those young parents
In their inexperience
Will always be deciding all decisions.

By now a second long nine months have passed,
and now at last is OUR time, heartbeat Danny.

Your eyes light up for me now
We growl a special growl at one another
And as I fell in love
One by one
Deep and forever
With my babies
(They were your uncles and your mother)
Now my Danny, Heartbeat,
Now it's you.

Croup
by Merle Feld

At night
in our bed
rigid
listening
listening for that breathing

And then
racing to the bathroom
hot water
steam

We take turns holding him — thirty pounds, fighting for air
together we hold him
(How does a single parent do this?)
the steam condensing on the three of us
I've never loved you more
than this moment
in our bathroom.

I don't let him feel my fear
I take all of his fear into me
and finally, the heavy little body relaxes
back into his crib.

I love you so much
I love you so much

And you God — I hate you
I hate you with all my heart
with my clenched teeth
with my clenched fists
with my fingernails I hate you
for playing with me and my little boy.

And you God — thank you
Thank you — I kiss your feet
You let me keep my little boy.
I'll be so good
You won't be sorry.

First published in Response, *1985.*

Prayers for a Sick Daughter
by Madeline Tiger
for Barbara Joan

i

I sleep
this winter
into your pain
I want to dream
deep   into the night garden
way under your flowering

I want to burrow until the inside
of my inside sac of my body/my mind
takes me back   and you will be
there with me
and I will move my hands
around your chilly body
your roots and tender parts
your blood tapping stilly
in the dark earth of us
your little fragile tissues
only my bathinette fingers
may touch. Oh I will hold you
inside the earth my baby
inside the womb so gently
so lightwarm as the evening bath
when then you first slept here
tiny fisted and rosy beside me
when hopeful and curious you allowed me
to wipe the night of your brow and
the wet stars from over your eyes

ii

Every night
I sleep into your pain
I go to sleep thinking into your pain
I go toward it to enter
                the form it has taken

in you
I want to dream it on
like the inside skin of my inside sac of
my body/my mind
Then when I wake up
you will be home free home free
running painless forever and ever

We are so strong
you are so strong
this will be soon
this will be done
you will be well soon

I love you

iii

I cannot find
the old place of adhesion
if only I could find
that spot of thick
where my flesh was your flesh and
my blood was your blood and I pumped what
you needed and I never forgot you
I never mistook you
I never overlooked you

and nothing was missing and nothing
could hurt you
and I cleaned your spleen and your liver
your lungs and your colon

152

your tubes and your ovaries
and our waters were rinsing
my juices were cleansing your juices
even when I was sleeping and
you may have been swimming, we were well
and the world was around us all starry,
all spinning

and then it was morning

iv

In here, baby, we will do libations:
touching and shaking little inches
Then we will part the soil
and you will be with me
Then I will lift my hands
and you will be in them
Then I will open my body
and you will be of me
Then I will move my legs
and you will be moving
Then I will raise you up
and you will be whole
and there will not be any pain
and your limbs will be free
of pain
and your skin will be warm
without pain
and your blood will flow
and your organs will pump
and your breath and your voice
and your mind and mine,
we will be done
to begin

Nine
by Elizabeth Zelvin

convenient, my darling
you being nine
this year that I'm sleeping alone
we have time in the long evenings
for the fears
that you are old enough to tell
young enough to trust your mother with

the books explain
why you at nine
go suddenly in terror of the dark
you who take the Broadway bus alone
and can scrub a pot until the metal shines
the books explain why nine's the age for weeping
because you can't cut up your lamb chop
why nine's the age you ask
what causes war
and weep again for fear you can't convince them
that you don't want to go

it's all in the books, my love
but you are real
your hair that smells of cucumbers when it's clean
your elf ears, still fluted from the birth canal
your body, sleek and downy
that I am still allowed to touch
as you float suspended in the bath

the books say I will have you for a little longer
before you curl into the shell of puberty
elusive, convoluted, slippery as a conch

how sad, my darling
when only since you're nine
have I had time to say

that I am lonely sometimes
and you've had wisdom
to say that people's feelings
are "sort of not your specialty"
and yet, when I cry
to put your arms around me

First published in I Am the Daughter, *New Rivers Press, 1981.*

Bar Talking
by Gayle Spanier Rawlings

for Pat and her children

Long ago — one time, many times,
we sat talking
into the dark smokey
air of our life
dreams,
you the sculptor,
I the dancer-poet.
You told me you would
never bring children
into this messy world,
and that we would go
to Mexico.
We never did,
and I saw your children
today.
Their eyes sparkle
with all the twinkle
left over from our
forgotten dreams.

© *Gayle Spanier Rawlings, 1989.*

Dayeni
by Shulamith Surnamer

Rebono,
        would it not have been sufficient
                      for me
to have cleaned my house for Pesach
   to have rid my home of all chametz
      to have carefully kashered the oven with a blowtorch
              and
        to have bought new clothes for the children I already have?
Rebono,
        would all this not have been sufficient
                      for me?

Must I,
       a woman expecting her eighth
                    Erev Pesach
also be blessed
        with a husband and children
                    allergic to wheat
who need me to
        hand grind and hand bake
                    matzas made out of oats?

tah shema
by Shulamith Surnamer

Come, Come and Listen
Rabbi Abahu
is speaking
with his fellow farmers
in far-off Palestine:
If you find
cut figs on the road
even if they are lying
next to a field full
of cut, drying figs
you can keep them.
It is not considered
robbery.

                    But,
if you find
an olive
or a carob
on the road
you can not keep it.

    Do we not all know
    just by looking at an olive
    just by looking at a carob
    on whose tree
    it grew?

Come. Come and Listen
Rabbi Abahu —
6th graders
are hearing
your words
in an American school
in a classroom
overlooking not
fields of growing fruit
but a boardwalk,
a beach of sand, an ocean
of days far different from yours;
eleven-year-olds
re-argue what to do
about *k'tzioos*, the fallen figs
tzaitim, the fallen olives
charoovim, the fallen carobs
and with Rashi's help
understand
you and your friends'
ancient languages
of agrarian ownership
of Aramaic discourse
of talmudic logic

as on back benches
parents pridefully lean forward
listening to their fruit
repeat your words:

> *Do we not all know*
> *just by looking at an olive*
> *just by looking at a carob*
> *on whose tree*
> *it grew?*

First published in New Traditions, *1986.*

Photo-Finish Brat
by Marion D. S. Dreyfus

i

About once a week, invited, I
visit my friend Louise who is
not only my best friend but the
mother of my second husband, and
when she goes to sleep   I
moon around looking for old *New Yorkers*
and op-ed articles I missed first time
around, a stack of pictures maybe a
deck tall pokes into my heart and
I pick the photos up and catch up on
the newest baby my second husband
now has, remarking how weary his third
wife looks, how scrawny this red-faced
latest seems to me (*mine* would be
angelic and Noh-drama snowy-white)
and peering at my once-husband, now
merely son-of-best-friend, note how very the
same he looks, save his face . . .
equivocal, not radiant, I ahh with
absolute satisfaction (*our* pictures
show him jealously hauling me tight
to his capacious chest, a smile so wide
it looks depicted by a court artist)
And I go through the pile once more, memorizing
the second child, now, hmm, 5½, and she's
really cute, a pixie I cannot imagine
having been produced by those . . .

ii
Pressing my
   nose against the
      window of their
marriage I
   hate their proof-of-
      the-pudding brat.

Hate her.

Mellowing then
   into my own
      pane or two I
glance idly across their
   grassy sprawl and recognize
      a half-grown child.

Either she's grown up.

Or I.

Nancy's Aliyah
by Cyrille Kane

Mother's annoying everyone again
Taking pictures out of focus at the airport
Discovering later what went wrong
Nancy is furious with me — a failure again.
I can't fix it for her in the hazy morning light
Will anyone notice when I disintegrate?

Partings
by Florence B. Freedman

Birthing (then) and (now) parting
Were harder than I have ever said.

When the time came for you to be born
You lay curled and quiescent . . .
For ten days I counted the hours
Until, stirring and thrashing,
You sent signals of pain to tell me
the time to let go had come.

    But my body refused.
    Its lips would not utter you . . .
    Steel widened a way.

You did not then plunge headlong into life,
But presented a testing hand.
Skilled hands turned you within me
And drew you forth.

Now at parting, again pain signals to me
It is time to let go.
    What wise hands will turn me about?
    What steel cut true,
    Leaving a thin scar?

Eyt Ziknah

Old People at the Film Series at the Museum of Modern Art
by Ruth Daigon

Every Monday, the city herds,
feeds and protects old people
like an endangered species.
The rest of the week it's open season.

When the bus unloads,
some move toward the entrance,
sniffing to see which way the wind blows.
Others inch along full of
leanings and complainings.

All week they've been detaching days
wrapped around each other
like cabbages, measuring time
by the coffee rings staining the table top.

Now each of them holds
in a marinated hand, a ticket
to an afternoon of shadows.

All through the movie,
they croon to themselves.
And when it ends, they climb
back on the bus, and settle into place
folding moments like clean wash.
Then they lick their lips, tasting
the sweet connection of their first ten years
together with the bitter flavor of the last.

First published in Greenfield Review, *1989.*

Louder, Please
by Florence B. Freedman

My psychiatrist, having turned eighty,
Has become a little hard of hearing.
I raise my voice and speak very clearly.

I pray louder too,
heaving heard that
God is deaf.

My Mother-in-Law's Name is Rose
by Helen Papell

You grasp your cane with the hunger
of a toddler to stand alone. Sometimes
you walk it step by step
to a grocery for yogurt, sometimes it points
to a village that was rubble long ago.

Do you remember the sting of leaf-green
from the village tree
filling your mouth like salt waves?

You tell me sounds are now sand dunes
dribbling into each other.
Your tongue tastes cardboard washed
upon a beach
instead of a goulash conjured
with secret spices,
your senses disappear one by one
following father, mother, husband, daughter.

Don't go yet, Rose.
Emblazon a decal sunflower upon a tee-shirt.
Mix a supermarket mustard sauce
to put green into a can of potato soup.
Stand, your name is still Rose.
Twirl your cane, stretch your arms,
let them tango.

First published in Up Against the Wall, Mother, *1986.*

Anna, My Mother-In-Law
by Merilee Kaufman

A left eye that squints,
gray straight, barrette-clipped hair.
White cotton socks in black slippers,
a decade old, meant for a man.
A nubby orlon sweater tucked into
zipper-broken plaid slacks,
held together by a long piece of wool.
A big smile that spreads across her face
when her family comes to visit.
A woman who gave her wedding band
and gold jewelry to her daughters-in-law
to enjoy.
Anna, my mother-in-law.

Weekly, she'd serve us
a full course dinner: melon, soup with
knedalach, chicken, a starch, a vegetable
fruit and nuts for dessert.

For her failing eyes, we'd clear places
on the table so she could
set the meal down.

"What else can I get you," she'd ask, "to nosh?"

This evening at our house she watches tv,
feet on a hassock, raised to reduce swelling.

After our day's work, the meal is simple.
She chooses noodles and cheese.
She cannot chew the salad.
"No dessert, thanks," she says.

When I tell her she's given me so much
and I can give so little, she asks,
"So when can I do it again?"

© *1986 Merilee Kaufman.*

Companions
by Michelle Bender

Sitting in the park
they exchange
an occasional word
that moves
between their gray heads
like the pendulum
of an old clock,
pauses —
in mid-air
until the weak chime
of memory
sounds
and is heard:
"Yes, I remember . . ."
"I wonder where . . ."

They tell stories
told before,
of people they've known,
another war,
travels,
a child's birth,
Then
smile
at each other,
nod in reply,
sigh;
Listening to another time
they do not hear
the bees nearby
gathering nectar
among the roses;
Instead
he shifts his seat,
opens his shirt,
closes
his eyes,
dozes,
starts to snore
while
she retreats
to the hum
of time
and the sundial
gathers shadows.

©Michelle Bender, 1986.

Erasures
by Ruth Daigon

i

I'm beginning to forget names, faces,
the day, the date, the year.
You grow impatient.
You say I'm irresponsible.
You appoint yourself my guardian.
You wear a tweed coat,
a fedora, a shoulder holster
like a secret service man.
You carry a net to catch me
when I fall from heights;
a rope to leash me
when I move too fast
or laugh too loud.
You tell me when to wake
and when to sleep.
You'll grow a beard
like a rabbi or a judge
and stroke it while you recite
my foolish stories.
Soon you'll write my poems
and read them
while I sit listening
in the back row.
You'll lie awake at night
rehearsing all my grievances.
My turn to sleep
while you stare into the dark.
And on my last day,
you'll be the one to go,
leaving me here —
living and forgetting.

ii

There is only this house,
this room, this field and a tree
pulling away from its roots.
On one wall, a window makes
a centerpiece for the eye
focused on single ray of sun.
A trickle of water
like a thin strand of wire
drips from the tap.
In the kitchen, a fly perches
on the rim of a bowl,
wings lifting   lowering
polish the silence.
And outside, the road curves
away from itself.
Light spreads its slow stain
around the empty coffee cup
and the quieter it is,
the slower time passes
as I listen to my breath —
the oldest sound I know.

Sclerotic
by Enid Dame

Sclerotic means the scars are all inside.
An almost too-convenient metaphor.
Our lives consist of what we choose to hide.

Sometimes we told the truth, sometimes we lied.
We fed each other myths, accepted lore.
Sclerotic means the scars are all inside.

Our notes in bottles washed out with the tide.
We were relieved they never struck a shore.
Our lives consist of what we choose to hide.

We sat in your house tense, preoccupied.
Can surfaces reflect what's at the core?
Sclerotic means the scars are all inside.

I watched your world shut down. I know you cried.
Your hand went blank. Your coat dragged on the floor.
Our lives consist of what we choose to hide.

You never asked for help. You had your pride.
Conspirator, I learned what to ignore.
Sclerotic means the scars are all inside.
Our lives consist of what we choose to hide.

First published in Pivot, *1985.*

Gray Hairs
by Naomi Replansky

Gray hairs
crowd out the black.
Not one of them
brings me wisdom.

Wrinkles
provide no armor.
I still quiver
to anyone's dart.

First published in The Dangerous World, *1989,*
© *Naomi Replansky.*

Therapist
by Ruth Roston

Marcia Fogelson is dancing
in the ward that stinks to heaven
of old children
strapped in wheelchairs. She is singing
them a brightness   words in Yiddish.
She is dancing   arms outstretched
across the urine   over feces.
Marcia Fogelson is rising
spinning light into the whiteness
of the ward.

The Hardest Work of All
by Madeline Tiger

and one week later
he was allowed to dangle
his legs over the edge
of the bed, was it a boat
my father rode back to life
in this casual manner, a towel
on his knees, a blanket
thrown over his shoulder,
the monitor tocking, an orange,
a tomato, his favorite coffee
arranged on the windowsill,
still, not his own roof,

the refrigerator down the hall,
her noodle soup on the shelf;
she fed him herself, watching him
master the bed, turn his legs under
the shifting table, Captain Bare-back,
electrically wired, still

no whisper of the visitor
who hadn't come this time, and Mother
was well-bred enough
not to show how tired
she felt steering him over
the beat of both hearts   saying
not yet   not yet

Published in The Chinese Handcuff,
© *1983 by Madeline Tiger.*

Houseguest
by Michelle Bender

Death lives in our house,
a guest
always there
who airily roams
the halls,
watching;
A quiet chaperone
to our love affairs
with life;
Like a faithful spouse
she waits
to meet,
Barely
catching
a glimpse of our heat
and lust,
does not intrude
from the cool corners
of our homes.

Then,
loyal wife,
she calls,
asks us
to play
host,
to prepare
for her stay;
So we shop,
wash dishes,
grab the broom,
sweep the dust,
cook the food
to share;

Then go to her room,
shut the door,
draw the drapes,
block out the day,
and wonder
when
we must
turn down the sheet.

© *Michelle Bender, 1986.*

Newark
by Madeline Tiger

Mrs. Lane
lives alone now
in the front room
are the mourners
and the nieces
in the kitchen
the pot boils
the torn shade
in the bedroom
is drawn down
most days
and going by
the room
in the middle
where he died
Mama   and the others
stop,   turn aside,
and sigh   like deer
in winter

First published in The Chinese Handcuff, *1983.*
© *Madeline Tiger.*

The Kohain's Wife
by Shulamith Surnamer

In the month of Av
month of mourning
my rabbi-father yet alive
but my mother
newly-gone . . .

        It is lonely to be
        the wife
        of a kohain
        at funeral time
        by myself I sit
        in the front row
        at the funeral chapel
        listening to the eulogy
        over my nearest flesh and blood
        knowing that my husband
        and sons
        are standing in the parking lot
        of the funeral home
        listening
        to the same eulogy
        piped over a loudspeaker
        outside
        just for them
        who may not be in the same room
        with death

In the month of Av
month of mourning
my rabbi-father yet alive
but my mother
newly-gone . . .

It is lonely to be
the wife
of a kohain
at burial time
by myself I stand
at the cemetery
under heaven's roof
shoveling back a last spadeful of earth
over my nearest flesh and blood
knowing that my husband
and my sons
are watching the earth
covering up
the plain pine coffin
from the paved cemetary roadway
under the same open skies
always
a ritually prescribed proscribed
four amot away
from death

First published in Shifra, *1986.*

Round
by Layle Silbert

In my head
house of bone
lie my mother my father
When I die
in whose head will I lie
& who will remember
my mother my father?

First published in West Branch, *1978.*

A Lifetime's Yizkor
by Miriam Bat Or

Too long have I mourned the passing of many springs
    barren of flowers.
But I have planted seeds for tomorrow
    and the autumn harvest is coming soon.

I had labored through a long dark winter,
    planted tulips and daffodils, lillies amaryllis and lilacs.
They bloomed gloriously for a moment:
    then a sudden frost chilled them to an early death.

Too long have I mourned the many losses of youth —
    the friends I might have made,
    the words I might have written,
    the songs I might have sung,
    the trees and skies I might have painted,
    the love and joy I might have given and received.

How long will I mourn for the husband who left me
    by taking his own life?
And now I mourn my mother's loss of her full powers,
    and I mourn for her pain.
Some day I will mourn for both mother and father.

And I mourn for the suffering of the oppressed
    and for the peace that might have been,
    and all those I might have saved from a bitter fate
    had not my youthful dreams been doomed.

Never will I cease to mourn.
The joy of the harvest to come will be bittersweet with
    mourning.
It is written, "There is a time to mourn and a time to dance,"
    but part of me is sobbing even while I dance.

A lifetime is too long a time to mourn,
   but for this was I meant from birth,
And from this will an ecstatic death, in the kiss of God,
   set me free,
When I will see my Beloved, after long and weary waiting
   for the glory of the heaven beyond the stars.

I never think of myself as waiting for you
by Merle Feld

I never think of myself as waiting for you
but then when the holiday has come and gone
when I'm packing up the Pesach dishes
or taking down the sukkah
I feel hopeless and alone

Inconsolable

Then I realize
I've left a small corner
somewhere deep inside myself
unpainted
And in that small corner
I'm still a child
a little girl
waiting

And I had hoped
without knowing it
that this *ḥag*
you'd come

My tears fall on the Pesach dishes
and I wonder
why you've left me here
alone

First published in Lilith, *1988.*

Elegy for My Father
by Henny Wenkart

And now — is the pain gone?
Sometimes I weep for you still.
But my Kiddush in your memory had the feel of celebration.
Your namesake dressed the Torah.

You were a young father
when you lost your father.
I remember the racking grief of your mourning.

Much later when your mother died
   that terrible grieving did not come again
I asked you about it and you said to me,
"I haven't closed the book."

Now, with the pain gone,
I think the reason may be

that I am beginning to open the book.

Kri'ah
by Henny Wenkart

Shall I put on this Kri'ah?

    The ragged black ribbon on a black button
    Funeral-parlor sackcloth
    That they give you at the graveside
    "Wear this for thirty days," the Rabbi says.
    You put it on
               and then they cut it
                         to show you
                                 that you are a
                                 mourner.

    To brand you a mourner.

Shall I wear — exhibit — this rag for my mother
who spent eighteen years dying?

And even — am I entitled?
Dare I wear it, who am implicated in her death —
Implicated in the form it had to take?

When once she felt herself going
she tried to die in dignity
and I
was an accomplice
of those who forced her to go on for years
becoming less
    And less
    And less —
Dare I put on a Kri'ah?

I decide to put it on,
Not for my merit
But hers.
And as the thirty days pass one day by one day
Am fortunate to wear it where people understand.
They ask, "What happened?"
"My mother died."
"Oh, I am sorry. May you be comforted among the mourners of Zion
    And Jerusalem."

And that is why.
I, a Jew, wear this Kri'ah
                      for her merit, not my own
And to give others the mitzvah of comforting the bereaved.

May you be comforted in the midst of — surrounded by —
the mourners for Zion and Jerusalem.

May you be comforted.

Ani Ma'amin

If
by Rose Gutman-Jasny

If another flood should come,
Let us, sisters all, from every land,
Say to God in his looming tower:

Whom are you hitting? Would you smite grasses
For their grassy sins? For the crooked paths
And dark tangles to which you destined them?
For their scanty roots which push toward earth,
Remote from your face?

If another flood should come,
We will take a dark view of it.
Let us, sisters all, from every land,
Say to God:
Turn back your punishing hand!

As a ravaged field cannot nourish seed,
So our deprived bodies will be sealed.
You'll conduct the Sabbath for desert winds
And smite the sea with thunder for its sins.

1939, United States.
Translated from the Yiddish by Etta Blum.

I cannot swim
by Irena Klepfisz

I cannot swim   but my parents
say the land is less safe.   And
the first day   the water was smooth
like slate I could walk on.
It was a deception.

The sky greyed   darkened
then grew bright   as if it understood
our mood.   I watched the land sink
and disappear.   The boat was firm.
I sat holding onto my father's leg.
I was not sick like the others.

The sky was bright   then grew
grey and dark. The days were
the same   the water the same
and everyone's eyes the same.
We looked like a family   but
we were all strangers. Nothing
but water and sky and the boat.
The world never existed I said.
I could not remember land   nor
houses   nor trees   and I knew
I had not been born here
that once there had been another place.
And I said to my parents:
there are no more lands
and no more peoples.   We are strange
creatures and must grow gills.
And my parents laughed as I cupped
my hands around my ears and the
children laughed and did the same
their bony fingers flapping.
And the water looked gentle
ready to receive us.

And one day   we saw them   and I
saw we were not alone   and there
were others. Not sea creatures
but like us. I remembered.
And they boarded us   and seized
the young girls like me   and formed
a circle.   And they were on us
when the leader shouted: Make
sounds of joy!   And my parents' eyes

sealed like wrinkled walnuts.
And they changed places   and new ones
were on us.   And someone ordered:
Make sounds of joy!   My parents moved
their lips   like fishes   their mouths
filled with silence.   And it happened
again and again   to me   till I stopped
remembering it.

The blood clotted between the boards
and darkened   though the women splashed
the sea on it. The smell stayed.
I said to my parents: I will grow gills
and tried to leap out   into the water.
But my father held my wrists   his fingers
iron nails piercing my bones.   And he said:
you cannot swim.

The ocean was bleak and jagged
like an unscaled mountain   daring
to be conquered.   At dusk someone
spotted the land   but I did not look
at it   and watched my shadow below
on the rippled darkening bottom.
I thought about those who waited
on the shore. They were shouting
sharp   not kind   pointing at an empty
horizon.   Wood splintered wood   just
for one moment   and then they pushed
us back.   My mother pressed my head
against her breast.   The day was ending.
It was almost dark.

First published in Sinister Wisdom *27, 1984.*

Abutilon in Bloom
by Irena Klepfisz

for Diana Bellessi

Cultivated inside   out of the bounds
of nature   it stubborned
on the windowsill   six winters and springs
resisting water   sun   all researched care.
It would not give   beyond its leaves.

Yet today   in the morning light
the sudden color asserts itself
among the spotted green   and I
pause   before another empty day
and wonder at its wild blooming.

It leans against the sunwarm glass
its blossoms firm on the thick stems
as if its roots
absorbed the knowledge
that there is no other place
that memory is only pain
that even here   now
we must burst forth with orange flowers
with savage hues of our captivity.

First published in Keeper of Accounts, *Sinister Wisdom Books, 1986.*
© *Irena Klepfisz.*

Childhood Memory
by Irene Grimberg

The place was Poland Warsaw
year 1939
The Germans ordered all Jews to wear
a special sign
an armband with blue star
most people thought it shame
my father brought two armbands
for mother and himself
Beautiful silken armbands
and on them a blue star

The white silk shone so brightly
bright was King David's sign
"How pretty they are," I thought
"I wish that I could wear one."

Hallo, Hallo . . .
by Cecile Low

Hallo, Reverend Mother? Hallo!
This is Madame Liliane Labió,
The mother of Marie-Henriette
To flee from here I am all set . . .
Thank you, Reverend Mother, yes . . .
I long for her, yes, I confess;
But I am glad she is with you . . .
With you she will be safe, it's true.
Her little brother, my son Ray,
Was unfortunately dragged away.
Among four thousand children he was
Seized by the French police, alas,
On this last July seventeen.
He was home with his sitter Jean.

The neighbors heard Little Ray's screams
But could do little, as it seems . . .
My son Ray is but three years old.
As my husband has been told,
All these Jewish children were
Kept in the Velodrome d'Hiver.
The police raided the whole city.
They did not show the slightest pity.
Into box cars the kids were thrown.
Their destination is not known.
Twelve thousand Jews were seized, oh woe!
Our French police did that, you know?
Who knows what still awaits us here.
We constantly live in such fear . . .
Yes, I know, we must all hope;
But with such things it's hard to cope!
I am so grateful to you, ma mère,
For all you've done, for all your care . . .
What is it? What did she do wrong? . . .
Forgive her this! She is so young!
May I talk with her a bit?
I will admonish her for it . . .
My Mirel, my joy, is that you?
Yes, my child, I love you too.
Now listen well what I will say.
I heard you wished to run away.
Why is it? Mirele, you should . . .
The institute is very good!
My Mirele, do not forget
That you are now Marie-Henriette . . .
Forget now that you are a Jew.
Your life you must save, Mirel, do! . . .
You will be baptized? . . . I wish you would!
Do all they want of you; be good!
The main thing is to stay alive.
God willing, I too will survive.
Then you will be with me again.
My Mirele, so long till then.

Laurie Drehmel

I Dreamed Him Homeward
by Yala Korwin

for E. K. whose brother went down with Struma

"The small steamer Struma, *with 750 Jewish refugees from Rumania and Bulgaria aboard, was blown to pieces in the Black Sea about five miles north of the Bosphorus, apparently by a stray mine. . . . There have been no reports of survivors."*

THE NEW YORK TIMES, FEB. 25, 1942

He came to say good-bye:
"My sheepskin cap fooled them,
they took me for their own.
The Iron Guard let me pass.
The others? From Prayer House
to slaughterhouse. Quartered. Hung.
One ship got through to Palestine.
There is hope. I'll go."

I dreamed him only from the knees down,
but knew it was my brother.
These elongated bones of youth,
so full of vigor,
yet wrapped in rotting flesh,
treaded the black-green water.

I was the raging sea.
It was my body that yielded
to spidery rolling of his limbs.
Walk, walk my brother,
I'll guide you where
you want to go! My voice was
a rumbling of waves.

A day after the dream,
a postcard, his hand: "We are
cooped here forever. No toilets.
Most are sick. The boat unseaworthy,
but the Turks wouldn't let us land."

Mother pressed the letter
to trembling lips:
"Thank God. He lives."

Walk, walk my brother
where you want to go.
No entry papers needed
anymore.

First Published in Midstream, *1989.*

Warsaw Carousel
by Cecile Low

Just outside the Ghetto wall
Is the merry merry-go-round
And on it children, big and small,
Ride and swing and bound.

Hunger and sorrow reign inside.
Inside, each life decays.
Inside the wall, our children die
Outside the music plays.

First Thoughts: On Liberation Day From a Concentration Camp
by Annette Bialik Harchik

I will leave my prison,
climb down from filthy bunks
tiered six layers high
and escape the drone of commands,
work details and whippings,

to give free reign
to my breath, and arms,
and sex,
and dance my steps of ecstasy
however slowly.

I will crawl out
from the corners
of this creviceless space
where my body has huddled
for countless days,
and stumble into the sunlight.

I who have dared to live to this day
Now dare to leave the darkness of this place.

Earrings
by Annette Bialik Harchik

A Bialik tradition back home was
for a woman to wear earrings
from birth to death.

Ears pierced in infancy were
adorned in string;
golden hoops for girlhood;
diamond studs with marriage.

When the trains pulled up
at Auschwitz
my mother was stripped, shorn, tattooed,
and commanded to leave her earrings
in a huge glitter pile of jewelry.

Under her wavy white hair
her lobes hang heavy,
the empty holes
grown shut.

First published in Ghosts of the Holocaust, *ed. Stewart Florsheim, Wayne University Press, 1989.*

Kol Nidre
by Rosa Felsenburg Kaplan

for an adolescent during the Holocaust

All the vows
And all the promises not kept
Because life was too short
Or too difficult,
Or we were too young,
Not wise enough, or too weak—
Let them be cancelled!

I remember being glad
To leave behind my friend and Europe.
When she told me how life was started,
She had sworn me to secrecy.
Now she would not have to know
That I had told our secret.

The choking void of unsaid farewells
Because we did not know
We were together for the last time—
Let it be closed!

Alice and Malka, twin cousins with whom I played,
And whom I wished I looked like,
And whose parents, I thought,
Must love them more than mine loved me—
"One time," said their mother. "They mostly took young
   girls . . ."

For the sins committed on them
Forgive us: *S'lach lanu, m'chal lanu, kaper lanu!*

The unsaid thanks
To those who gave to us,
Life, sometimes,
But to whom we could not give —
Let thanks be understood!

Twice I took another's name
To cross a border.
What happened to my namesakes?

And to Onkel Michel,
And Tante Esti,
And Kati Neni —
Who took me in, housed me and fed me,
And whom I loathed and made fun of
Because they were not my parents,
Nor like them . . . ?

The tears unshed
Because we were too busy living
To mourn —
Let them now flow!

Trying to finish high school
And enter college,
Becoming American —
I shut my eyes to my parents' fears,
My heart to their losses as well as to my own. . . .

To those of us who live,
To our families and friends,
And all of those whom we're supposed to love —
Father of mercy,
Give them life
And us, time enough
To make peace,
Perhaps even to love them.

First published in Shirim, *1982.*

Twilight Zone
by Mindy Rinkewich

Of course the restaurant was open
Someone had to be there to give me a cup of tea
After hours of wandering through my mother's home town.

I bought a souvenir in a tiny store just before closing time
They had to run out and change a small bill to make change
I don't think anyone ever buys anything there
I had the feeling that after I left
They closed down the store
And the rest of the town.

First published in The White Beyond the Forest, *Merrick, 1989.*

Four Jewish Syrian Daughters
by Ada Aharoni

Written in commemoration of the four Syrian Jewish girls who were raped, murdered and mutilated when they tried to flee from Damascus Ghetto, February 1974.

My four sisters
The blood that flowed from you
Was my blood too,
The misuse of you,
The dismembered members
Were mine too

I heard him grin at Damascus Gate,
From this one I shall break
A breast,
From this her shapely leg
And small white ear,
From that a Jewish arm
And a cleft,
And from this one,
She is so pretty —
Just a tongue

If you see my Syrian sisters weeping in Damascus Ghetto,
Tell them
Their daughters' tongues
Have been grafted onto mine.

First published in Sephardic Views, *1989.*

Kiddush Levana
by Ruth Finer Mintz

blessing the new moon . . . Haifa, July
for Saul, nineteen years, fallen June 1967.

A thousand lamps for you in the curve of the shore
shaping below, the blessing,
for the pulse of the sea is the constancy of our longing.
Our masts are for you, torches,
as we stand on the watchtowers of longing.

Come to us out of the shadows, out of the circles of
mourning.
Lost, lost to parents, to friends. Lost, lost to the
beloved.

Come to us over water, for the stars are a gust of gulls
calling.

The sea ablaze is a rim of silver.
The sky ablaze is a rim of crystal.

Return us to yourself and we return
past the cup of salt and sorrow
to You, who are wine and water.

In the open places we set tables.
In flagons of pomegranate we store velvet fire.
For our desire has ripened, apricot and almond.
Our children eat, grow beautiful on the mountain.

First published in Jerusalem Poems, Love Songs, *Masada Press, 1976.*

Thinking About the Future of Jerusalem
by Shirley Kaufman

There is a black thread
winding around my legs
as on a spool strong as the thread
that's used to sew on gold buttons.
I can't break it off with my teeth.

That's what I get
for walking around in this city
with its excess of wars
and walls that go down deeper
than we can uncover.

I'm like a child
who lives only with adults,
They take her everywhere
in grown-up company
where she has to behave

when all the time
she wants to be singing
to herself or chasing
lizards running in and out
of the tall grass.

I have never seen a rock crumble
under the weight of history
or a life crumble
under the weight of fear.
And if I can only get

My legs untied I'll stand
in line with all the people
who eat too much at buffet tables
and keep filling filling
their plates with more.

The Letter I Wanted to Write, The Letter I Wrote,
for Osnat, an Ethiopian Student in Israel
by Dina Elenbogen

In the Medinah, in Marrakesh
a veiled girl tried to sell me a basket
she wove in greens, purples and the color of wheat.
Heavy lipped, black alabaster, like you
she stumbled through my language
pleading 20 dirham, 15 dirham . . .

**EVERYTHING IS FINE IN AMERICA.
I AM TEACHING AT THE UNIVERSITY.
I JUST GOT BACK FROM A VACATION FAR AWAY
NOT FAR FROM WHERE YOU WERE BORN.
YESTERDAY IT RAINED SO HARD
THERE WERE RIVERS IN THE STREETS.**

The veiled girl grabbed my wrist
with her slender fingers
chanting 10 dirham, 5 dirham . . .
When I walked away I saw your eyes
large wooden bowls, waiting
to be filled.

**ARE YOU HAPPY IN YOUR NEW COUNTRY?
ARE YOU STUDYING VERY HARD?
ARE YOUR BROTHERS AND SISTERS STILL WITH YOU?
DOES YOUR MOTHER FEEL BETTER
NOW THAT THE RAINS HAVE PASSED?
I AM SORRY. I CANNOT SEND MONEY.**

In the Medinah there were rugs
the colors of mountains and sky
and baskets in the bony arms of girls
like your thin legs that carried you
from Ethiopia to Sudan
and then to the place that was promised.

**HAS THE DREAM COME TRUE?
CAN YOU WRITE IN THREE LANGUAGES? SING
"BY THE WATERS OF BABYLON" IN ENGLISH?
I HAVE NOT STOPPED HUMMING THE WORDS.
MY STUDENTS ARE LEARNING POETRY
BUT DO NOT TAKE IT OUTSIDE THE ROOM.**

My students have golden pens.
They do not braid my hair in summer.
They run circles not knowing
of smaller countries
empty plates, washing in rivers
the sun asleep in fallow fields.

**DO YOU STILL WEAR THE BLUE BEADS
I GAVE YOU?
EVERYTHING IS OKAY IN AMERICA.
I HOPE YOU ARE WELL.
PLEASE EXCUSE MY LANGUAGE.
I HAVE ALMOST FORGOTTEN IT.**

I bought the basket from the girl
whose eyes shone through her white veil.
She wanted me to have another
but it was dusk
my arms were full
I pressed the coins to her palm.

**I AM SORRY.
I CANNOT SEND MONEY.
IT IS NOT EASY.
IT DOES NOT GROW ON TREES.
I PROMISE I WILL VISIT.
NEVER STOP WRITING.**

I filled the basket
with dirty clothes
and brought them back to America.
In the basement I hear them spin
and dream of rivers
cleansing orange against wheat.

Beta Israel
by Annette Bialik Harchik

Isolate sepia people dying slowly,
proud in your Sabbath laws.
Seed of Moses perhaps or Solomon,
descendants of Dan's tribe?

Will no one hear your pleas?
Your many numbered Jewish brothers,
when once you thought there were none,
they do not really listen.

And who will say Kaddish
after the last of you has died
diseased or starved or beaten.
To whom will you teach your Jewish ways,
strangers as you are even to your own kin?

First published in Response, *1987.*

Passover 1988
by Helen Papell

I'm of the tribe of Sarah
and Abraham; I say Sarah first
because men still name our boundaries.
This Passover Jewish women stack guns
like twigs of the burning bush,
Arab women gather rocks
once flung at Goliath.
I smell a pillar of cloud
above tires burning in the street.
Does a new Pharaoh tell Arabs to be quiet
while making bricks
for skyscrapers they can't live in?

Clubs cracking bones throwing stones:
>   Dare I dream
a daughter pulling an enemy child
from this river?

First published in Genesis 2. *1988.*

The Last Person Out of the Country, Please Turn Off the Lights
by Dina Elenbogen

The women, (hair wrapped in colorful scarves,
plastic baskets hanging from their wrists),
invade the market like hawks.
Tomorrow, everything doubles.
Bat Sheva gets enough toilet paper
to last until the next wind storm, like all of us
buys her bread fresh each day.
I grab tomatoes with the least bruises.
Someone rushes off quickly to another city,
our mail undelivered days.

Tomorrow the country just may close down.
The country is angry at itself
for the price of next week's meat
for the split party
for the love of our neighbors
for their desire to destroy us
for our need to destroy our neighbors
for the black children with mismatched skirts
for the black children with skull covers
for the stones that are thrown at them
for the stones that were thrown at us
for the black children with different prayers
for the black children with extra skin
between their legs.
The country is ashamed of itself
for giving in

for not giving back
for the absence of cigarettes
on storefront shelves, between
lips, under tables, for the emptiness
between its fingers.

The whole country threatens to stop tomorrow.
The Hasidim will throw their prayer books at the flies
beggars will close their fists on Rabbi Kook Street
buses will stop on the Hill of Evil Counsel
a man and a woman will pull apart
before finishing, a letter will stop
in the middle of the sea on the way
to someone's heart. The cats will land
inside trash cans and never come out.
Tomorrow everything, the trees too,
will lie down in exhaustion,
everything except the wind
opening and slamming doors,
everything but the doors creaking like age
everything but the flies finding their way
back to us, everything but the flies,
devouring what is already lost.

Maalot, Israel (after a national strike).

Nachamu

Seasons of Torah

i

Pale moon,
ever coming and going,
lighting and fading
rhythmic flowing
signal of new time and changing seasons,
awaken in us
the mystery of beginnings and endings,
of lives renewed.
Awaken us to the beauty of endless cycles
visible signs of God's eternal love.

Nancy Lee Gossels

ii

Somewhere out of time
In the mystery of time
Somewhere between memory and forgetfulness,
Dimly though
I remember how once I stood
At Your mountain trembling
Amid the fire and the thunder.
How I stood there, out of bondage
In a strange land and afraid.
And You loved me and You fed me
And I feasted on Your words.
And, yes, I can remember
How the thunder was my heart
And the fire was my soul.
O God, I do remember.
The fire burns in me anew.
And here I am, once more
A witness to that timeless moment,
Present now in the light of Your Torah.

Nancy Lee Gossels

iii

The ark is sweet with flowers' scent.
The moon is full with expectation.
We are come with sleepless eyes
to study and to pray. The hours of the night
invite us; the Torah waits for our embrace.
Awake, my soul,
and feast on dreams
of mystery and wonder,
then in the haunting shadows rise
to receive once more the breath of Light
in the whispered awakening of dawn.

Nancy Lee Gossels

iv

Unroll the parchment scroll.
Hold it gentle like a child.
Unfold your portion to you; draw it close.
Let its story dance the circle of the room,
Unbroken words from voice to voice,
Letters soaring from the Torah of our hearts.

Here, where the end embraces the beginning,
Like eternal bride and bridegroom joined as one,
Rejoice!

Nancy Lee Gossels
Joan Kaye
Rosie Rosenzweig

First published in Vetaher Libenu,
by Congregation Beth El of the Sudbury River Valley, 1980.

I Know Not Your Way
by Malka Heifetz Tussman

I know not your ways —
A sunset is for me
a Godset.
Where are you going,
God?
Take me along,
if, in the "along,"
it is light,
God.

I am afraid of the dark.

1949, United States.
First published in Am I Also You, *Tree Books, 1977.*
Translated from the Yiddish by Marcia Falk.

Sabbath Eyes
by Nancy Lee Gossels

i

Holy One of Being,
Help us replace
The earthbound things,
Confines of space,
With Sabbath eyes,
With Sabbath heart.

Help us to climb,
To reach that place
In sacred time
Where we can find
Our Sabbath soul.

Help us, we pray,
To recognize
Your Holiness,
To sanctify
And to embrace
The Sabbath day,
Your precious gift,
With love and grace.

ii

O God, we come before You, a diverse assembly,
A patchwork of pressures and anxieties.
Many of us are tired.
Many of us are alone.
Many of us feel imprisoned
By the shackles of the weekday world.
Refresh us.
Comfort us.
Free us.
Help us to make that hard passage
From time past to time now.
Help us to live in Your presence.
Help us to find peace,
The eternal promise of Shabbat.

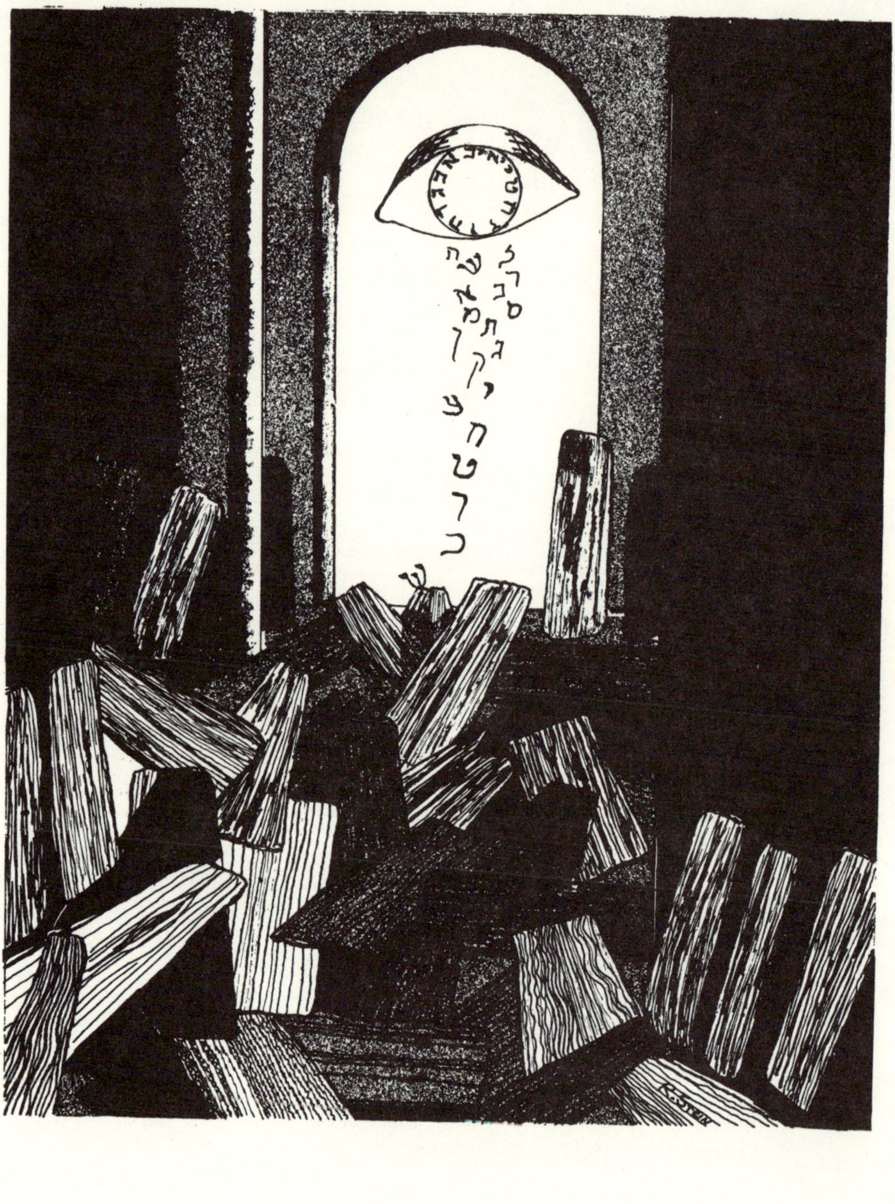

iii

We are like helpless boards of wood.
We are like eyeless panes of glass.
You are the mighty Oak, Creator.
You, the Source of all light streaming.
You, the Architect of beauty.
Yours, the blueprint of Creation.

Without You, our lives are hollow.
We are soulless, sawdust only,
Thirsting for the truth of Torah.
Yet when You're near, a room becomes
A holy place where souls can soar.

Just as the beauty of the ark
Springs from the precious scrolls it holds,
So we, too, dignify our days
When we embrace Your treasured words,
The essence of Your lasting love.

Be with us now and hear our prayer.
Bind this congregation to You.
Fill us with the light of Torah.
Help us feel Your presence always.

First published in the Siddur Vetaher Libenu *by Congregation Beth El of the Sudbury River Valley, 1980.*

The Maabaroth
by Rikudah Potash

Good evening, Lord God,
I have a prayer to you,
Lord God,
For our Maabaroth.

It is not enough
That our people come
From horror and from blood,
It is not enough that they come to us,
To live in Maabaroth.
It is not enough, Lord God!

Their Ark is smaller than Noah's Ark.
And no dove comes to their door.
What comes is the rain beating down on their roofs,
Beating down in a steady pour.

What comes is the wind, cold as ice,
Biting into their bones.
In all the Maabaroth, Lord God,
You hear children's cries and old people's groans.

Give them strong roofs and walls, Lord God,
And windows to let in light,
Shield them from the wind and rain,
Give them comfort in the night.

Circa 1925, Israel.
Published in The Golden Peacock, *Thomas Yoseloff, 1961.*
Translated from the Yiddish by Joseph Leftwich.

In This Galaxy Flowing with Milk and Honey
by Shulamith Surnamer

Are we Jews sentenced to stay
only on this small ball of space
bound to this earth
this ancient planet
like one entire vast
Promised Land?

Where is there the expert
on extraterrestrial halacha
to tell a new generation
of wandering Children of Israel
how to light the Shabbes licht
while orbiting
the galactic desert
for countless lightyears
in a place where there is
no day, no night?

Where is there the Rabbinic Sage
the Gaon of Ganymede
able to explain, to expound
to a stiff-necked group
how to celebrate the new month
how to mark a Rosh Chodesh
on a planet with two moons
or three moons
or no moon at all?

There is no Sanhedrin on Saturn
no Bet Din of the Big Dipper
to teach the faithful
far-flung remnant

how to observe a Yom Kippur
a Chanukah, a Purim, a Pesach
on a celestial sphere
remote from the Torah's origination
tied to Terra's turns
beneath Earth's Sun
beneath Earth's Moon.

I lift up my voice
unto the mountains
from whence
oh from whence will come
the prophetic voice
to reveal God's Command
This is how to keep Shabbes
even on Uranus
not like one lost
on desert sands
forced to start anew
a seven day cyclical count
making each uncertain day
a semi-shabbat
doing only what is necessary
for survival
and differentiating every 7th day
with the saying of Kiddush
over what little water is at hand

This day is the real Sabbath Day
will some new Jeremiah
from Nueva Jerusalem II thunder
Make it Holy
with the juice
of an indigenous vine
under the hechsher
of home-grown Ḥachamim.

First published in Chesapeake Shalom, *1985.*

Sabbath
by Helen Papell

I have chopped the fish
with a wooden knife in a wooden bowl,
as Grandma Hanah taught me,
    carp and whitefish from the peddler's ice,
    eyes red
    gills still shivering.
The broth has jelled.
              Come, my sister.

I have sprinkled salt on the chicken
spread open upon a wooden block,
as Grandma Leah taught me,
    I heard it scream
    I pulled the feathers
    and singed the skin.
Its blood has dried.
              Come, my sister,
              the garden is waiting.

Your candlesticks are on the warm stove
in my darkening kitchen,
as Mama taught me,
    and on the table for my children
    bread I kneaded
    wine I squeezed.
Tomorrow, I need not kill.
              Come, my sister,
              the garden is waiting
              blue blossoms hang low
              on the bush.

© The Jewish Frontier, *1982*.

Paean After Snow
by Louise Jaffe

And lo it came to pass
After her feet had been jailed
In those black suede
Fleece-lined cells
Called boots
For a ten-day
    slip-slide
Sentence,
An early-February January thaw
Changed blustering-bully
To don't-take-me-seriously
Snow
And it was good.
And lo it came to pass
That inchingly
She unzipped her feet to freedom
And they made friends
With shoes again
And it was good.
And lo the feet and shoes went walking
Up and down
The puddling streets
And it was good.
And though the shoes were gum-soled
                      black-laced
                      workaday
Oxfords
The feet
Thanksgivingly
Felt almost as if they were making love
To the earth
And it was good.
And lo it came to pass
That little electric ripples
Travelled up those feet

To the legs
   the loins
      and finally the heart
Helping it believe
Even in this pre-green time
That there is such a thing
As spring
And it was good.
And the owner of the boots
                shoes
                feet
                legs
                heart
And shivers of wintry doubt
Almost flew
On wings of swift belief
And it was good
So warmly, warmly good.
Amen.

First published in Wisdom Revisited: Athena Speaks, *Adams Press, 1987.*

Birdsong & Sun Poem for Winter
by Madeline Tiger

a sparrow hops in the lilac on the arab side of our house.
sun surrounds his round body.
his feathers close on the dark
center.
he faces winter, and the sun-line around him
from the distant east
holds him bright through frost.
all the needles shiver on our southern firs.
in the deciduous north
the young honey locust,
a thin tree,
raps against a brick chimney.
December will be windy.
we are protected to the west
by a double pane of glass.
there are also the motionless junipers.

First published in Penumbra, *1972.*

Tu B'Shevat
by Annette Bialik Harchik

Midwinter yet it has started.
Rain waters soak tap roots.
Days begin to lengthen.
Earth's long pull starboard
towards the sun recommences.

It is altogether
a commencement of the earth.
Under Shevat's full moon
the sap rises.
And what was once as frozen
as transparent ice
shows buds beginning
      blossoms.

First published in Response, *1987.*

The Sun and I
by Rachel Fishman

I am sunned
sunned through
sunburnt.

Burst me open:
sunflower seed
will pop from my center.
I swallow so much sun
I laugh and mirror
sun signals.

Though my every corner sees the light
I am not afraid.
Full of sunlight,
it is one to me
whether I shine forth

or receive the light.

Translated from Yiddish by Shulamis Yelin.

Sunflowers
by Dina Elenbogen

The sunflowers are turning
their heads, they are bowing out,
wilting away between the sea
and the Arab villages, the Arab villages
and the Moroccan town where I live.
I want to quench them.

I want the rain to fall
but the sun gets crueler each day.
If I had buckets full of water
I couldn't save them.   I know I couldn't.
That's why I sit here speechless, like the day
I watched the fires spontaneously

erupt outside the buildings
where the Ethiopians live.
The fireman came with a yarmulke and cigarette.
He was as dry as desert.
He lit fire to all the land
until there was nothing left to burn.

I had wanted to pick those flowers,
for the Sabbath, I had wanted to
place them on the kitchen table
next to the candles, bread and wine.
I had dreamt of keeping them whole.
And when I couldn't bear them anymore

I'd empty them, toss the seeds to the birds.
There are beautiful birds here
and beautiful sky.   Someone reached
his hand out the window and caught one.
He said he didn't mean, his hand
larger than the blue bird's body.

Because it was Shabbat,
he threw the poor bird up through the hole
in the ceiling and freed him.
Shabbat is no day to kill, even the sun-
flowers.   Shabbat is too long with so much sun,
too long without flowers, with broken wings.

Maalot, Israel, 1985.

221

Bible Students In The Sukkah
by Barbara D. Holender

What does it matter
that we are forever looking things up
and forgetting them?
Our minds are like the sukkah:
crowned with evergreen
open to the stars and winds
hung with our best fruits
and reconstructed each year.

The pine boughs shake down sun,
the leaves of our books cast up light,
and all our ancestors
cluster around us, saying
This is who we were
and *this* is what we did
and *this* is what it meant.

So it must have been at Pumbedita
in ample Babylon
where our Talmudic fathers
from every jot and tittle
extracted meanings
and over golden dates and wine
discoursed on the family tree

and one always had a story,
and one always said, Be serious.

© *Barbara D. Holender*
Winner of Hans S. Bodenheimer Award for Poetry, 1984.

The Crossing
by Patricia Moger Varshavtchik

I have searched, delved, studied.
I have immersed myself.

The bridge glistens
Reaching out across the Straits.
The waves stretch from silver through jade to deep blue.

In the house on the other side,
    Grandmother quilts pattern the walls,
    And handsewn pillows fill the chairs.
    There is blueberry banana cake,
    And blackberry tea in delicate, painted cups.
I am questioned simply,
"How did you come to this?"
My thoughts unwind themselves into words.
Intent and focused is the response in their faces,
Joyful and warm.
Understanding and welcome dance between us.

As I choose my name,
The water of the Lake rests nearby,
Sparkling.

We All Stood Together
by Merle Feld

for Rachel Adler

My brother and I were at Sinai
He kept a journal
of what he saw
of what he heard
of what it all meant to him

I wish I had such a record
of what happened to me there

It seems like every time I want to write
I can't
I'm always holding a baby
one of my own
or one for a friend
always holding a baby
so my hands are never free
to write things down

And then
as time passes
the particulars
the hard data
the who what when where why
slip away from me
and all I'm left with is
the feeling

But feelings are just sounds
the vowel barking of a mute

My brother is so sure of what he heard
after all he's got a record of it
consonant after consonant after consonant

If we remembered it together
we could recreate holy time
sparks flying

First published in the Reconstructionist Siddur, Kol Haneshamah, *1989.*

Yiddish
by Layle Silbert

on the second anniversary of Liberation
the Polish consul in Shanghai
gave a garden party in Hongkew
here Jews stayed alive
during the war by not being in Europe
a bearded rabbi with blue eyes
spoke to me in local dialect
I shrugged   smiled
he spoke in Polish   then Russian
tried German

suddenly in the hot summer air of China
in the sweet flow of a forgotten spring
I found my mother tongue
rapturous   I answered in the common language
we'd both been born into
in Poland   in America
I laughed at his accent
he laughed at mine   Lithuanian
learned from my father
it didn't matter

The Influence Coming into Play: The Seven of Pentacles
by Marge Piercy

Under a sky the color of pea soup
she is looking at her work growing away there
actively, thickly like grapevines or pole beans
as things grow in the real world, slowly enough.
If you tend them properly, if you mulch, if you water,
if you provide birds that eat insects a home and winter food,
if the sun shines and you pick off caterpillars,
if the praying mantis comes and the ladybugs and the bees,
then the plants flourish, but at their own internal clock.

Connections are made slowly, sometimes they grow
    underground.
You cannot tell always by looking what is happening.
More than half a tree is spread out in the soil under your feet.
Penetrate quietly as the earthworm that blows no trumpet.
Fight persistently as the creeper that brings down the tree.
Spread like the squash plant that overruns the garden.
Gnaw in the dark and use the sun to make sugar.

Weave real connections, create real nodes, build real houses.
Live a life you can endure: make love that is loving.
Keep tangling and interweaving and taking more in,
a thicket and bramble wilderness to the outside but to us
interconnected with rabbit runs and burrows and lairs.

Live as if you liked yourself, and it may happen:
reach out, keep reaching out, keep bringing in.
This is how we are going to live for a long time: not always,
for every gardener knows that after the digging, after the
    planting,
after the long season of tending and growth, the harvest comes.

First published in Circles on the Water, *Knopf 1982.*

Haj
by S. Ben-Tov

Toward evening, the sun has fired
the sky to a glaze so violet hard
an airplane's drone would crack it,
rim to rim.

I walk to the city's edge,
past children playing in the balconies
and open doors,
my bare soles pressing
the warm, moldable tar
with its sweet, tired smell.

Through the streets the white sun drops to red,
the white light snaps,
and the city fills with rose,
trembles, seems to rise;
only a few black cypresses,
like tent pegs, hold it down.

I pick a path across a field
of gray, star-spiked thorns, purple nettles,
and tumbled barbed wire.
Here, from time to time,
old buried mines are triggered
by a stray goat's step:
the whole city hears the puncture.

Long lines of alfalfa
are planted in a clearing, where I wait.
The dry ground is still hot:

up shoot white rows of fountains
with double wings —

across the field, the water pipes are singing.

From the long poem "During Ceasefire", *first published in* During Ceasefire, *by Sharona Ben-Tov. Reprinted by permission of Harper & Row, Publishers, Inc. © 1985 by Sharona Ben-Tov.*

Qiryat Shmoneh
by Esther Cohen

Bible men walk
  with beards
  and green young daughters
through new stores
filled
with beds of beans and nuts
and winter oranges.
I watch them,
carrying the Galilee
in cotton nets with Sabbath bread.
They are all neighbors;
they hide their knees
with Persian flowers
they sit in the sun
and pound their stones
to seeds of dirt
to Persian flowers
for their knees.
Once on Shabbat,
I watched them
eat soup
all together
   with a small golden spoon.
In school the children are dark and strong
their eyes hold the sun
while they laugh in their chairs.
Always they question,
tell me the Beatles
tell me the hippies
tell me why
you don't live forever
with us and the land and the hills and the sky.
Soon I tell them, my hair will reach Persia
my skin will smell oranges, my eyes will hold sun,
and I will become the Galilee and live on a mountain
on top of the sunrise and we'll eat soup together
   with one golden spoon.

Sarah's Daughters

Tsirl Waletzky

Holy Grandmothers in Jerusalem
by Esther Raab

Holy grandmothers in Jerusalem,
May your virtue protect me.
The smell of blossoms and blooming orchards
I suckled with my mother's milk,
Feet soft as hands fumbling
In the torrid sand,
And tousled eucalypti
Laden with bees and hornets
Whispered a lullabye to me.
Seven times shall I steep myself
In the Mediterranean
To prepare for King David, my beloved,
And I shall go up to him, with glorious dignity,
To the mountains of Jerusalem;
I shall sit with Deborah under the date-tree,
Have coffee with her and talk
About war and defense.
Holy grandmothers in Jerusalem,
May your virtue protect me.
I can feel the smell of your garments,
The aroma of Sabbath-candles and naphthalene.

1930, Palestine.
Translated from Hebrew by Abraham Birman.

A Letter to the Sons of Abraham
by Marcia Falk

Millennia have swept across the sands
Of Canaan, where your father Abraham
First cut the covenant, and you began
To carve out history with your own hands.

Consecrating time in weeks and moons,
You give it names and mark the holy days.
Because you have no inner moons to root
You to the earth, you find another way.

We, the daughters of Sarah, still bear sons
In labor for your laughter, and are banned,
When bearing only blood, from drawing near
Your altars with our exiled, longing hands.

But miracles will root within the soil
That holds the seeds of all exiled desire:
A candelabrum blooming in a field
Of pomegranate trees inscribed by fire —

The blazing letters flying from the leaves
And peeling from the bark in graphic forms
Like uterine linings folding back to earth
And down to deeper roots to be reborn.

The Girls That are Wanted
by Marie Odlum

The girls that are wanted are good girls—
    Good from the hearts to the lips;
Pure, as the lily is white and pure
    From its hearts to its sweet leaf tips.
The girls that are wanted are home girls—
    Girls that are mother's right hand;
That father and brothers can trust too,
    And the little ones understand.

Girls that are fair on the hearthstone,
    And pleasant when nobody sees;
Kind and sweet to their own folks,
    Ready and anxious to please.
The girls that are wanted are wise girls,
    That know what to do and say;
That drive with a smile and soft word
    The wrath of the household away.

The girls that are wanted are girls with hearts;
    They are wanted for mothers and wives;
Wanted to cradle in loving arms
    The strongest and frailest lives.

The clever, the witty, the brilliant girl
    There are few who can understand;
But, Oh! for the wise, loving home girls
    There's constant and steady demand.

1897, United States.

Minor Surgery
by Marion D. S. Dreyfus

During the procedure
   I thought of sex,
    My latest episode —
       Snugly nestled against my loin-memory only
         Hours before the knife.

As the anaesthetic ebbs,
   so does all thought of sex.
     Subsides, settles: Was it ever there?

Away from the surgical table
    Though young
  I walk all halt and reedy,
      Favoring my internal grief.

Throbbing, my blood pulses
    Endlessly:
    What have you done to us?
      To me?

With new eyes I empathize with age.
With gentle, closed smile, commiserate
      with the unwhole.
       With piercing recognition see the chasm
    Between once-well and
        seconds-later unwell.

I shy from the harmless
    Electric eyeful grazing
        Of soul-sucking cock-eyed males
I admit I usually seize and tease:

Will he demand from my
    Recuperative self
        What I have not to give?

My private face
    Is sunshadowed with doubt:
    (Whispery — *I cannot give* . . .
      I do not have . . .
Come back another day.)

When I am better.

God Only Knows
by Malka Heifetz Tussman

Like a worried mother
who has just weighed her child,
I stand bent over myself,
shaking my head:
That's not it,
that's not it,
and God only knows
if anything will ever
come of it.

1949 Israel and U.S.
Translated from Yiddish by Marcia Falk.

The Act of Bread
by Ruth Whitman

Some practice is required to knead quickly, but the motion once acquired will never be forgotten.

"Water Bread," The Boston Cooking-School Cookbook *by Fannie Merritt Farmer, 1898*

That happy multiplying
should have lasted all night.
But long before dawn
my batter crawled up the walls.
The trouble was, I let my secret
passion run into my thumbs:
into my own
flour yeast water I plunged my lust
up to the elbows — pounding the white
buttocks of my children, turning
their rosy heels; kneading the
side, loin, groin of him
to whom I long owed this caressing.

But before I could give form to desire,
invented flesh outran me.
It towered in my biggest bowl,
flowed over table shelves floor
till I scooped it up, frightened at my power,
and tried to hide it in a paper
bag. In an hour
it burst the side, climbed
out the window, through the door.
If I had baked that dough,
a crumb would serve as aphrodisiac:
one slice of bread
would people a continent.

      But in panic
I carried it outside, bucket by bucket,
and gave it to the cold November morning.

First published in The Marriage Wig and Other Poems, *Harcourt Brace Jovanovich, 1968.*

I Know About the Woman Who Sits and Waits
by Judith Rose

I know about the woman
    who sits and waits
  who sits and waits for her life
              to begin:

I know about the young girl who sits with her mother
    who sits and waits
         for her father
             to come

I know about the young woman who sits and waits
    who sits and waits
         for her lover
             to come

    I know about the woman who sits and waits
      who sits and waits
           for her husband
               to come

    I know about the woman who sits and waits
      who sits and waits
           for someone/something
                to come

I know about the woman who sits and waits
    who passes the waiting
                  onto her daughter

I know about the daughter who sits and frets
    who frets about more than time
                  misplaced

I know about the daughter longing for change
    who can/   no longer/   sit and wait
I know about the daughter longing for change
    who gives her Self the gift of
                  meaning full spaces

I know about the daughter longing for change
    who hopes for her daughter
                not
                    to sit and wait

© 1975 Judith Rose.

Parve
by Nina Judith Katz

There I was and I was parve
like my vegetarian meals
at their purest.
You can mix me with meat.
You can mix me with milk
I fit in with both   but
I am   neither.
Please honor me
for
although they claim that I do not offend them,
although they grudgingly grant me space on their plates
an unwanted reminder
of their fatty excess
although meat regards me as
its promised mate
and milk as its
primordial forbear
yet neither believes
I can stand on my own.
Each claims that I lack
my own essence.
They do not acknowledge
that I am fulfilling
all by myself
without them.
Still less do they hear
my cry of repulsion
at sharing their plate,
the Complement.

But a whispered conviction
straightens my spine
cracking the bones
and murmuring sweetly
in natural, honest and fair
bigotry:
I am more worthy than they
for I have killed no one
usurped no one's place
nor uprooted a plant
without tending the soil.
So kindly take your grease
off my plate
and
grant me
my own set of dishes.

Risa
by Marcia Falk

When Risa crosses her long legs
the length of her
a lovely shyness on the couch
softens all the corners in the room

but when she lets down
her kerchiefed hair
all the wadis of Judea go streaming
in the rush of spring

light river
by Marion D. S. Dreyfus

the other women watching
me enter the dark
winding
park road
call out to me— *Oh!*

there are no lamps
on this lane

only hurtling shapes
 loom black
whatever colors they
gleam by day

faith is my
handhold;
that I will find
my steadfast
footing
see my way
the half-mile
through

quickstepping
my footfalls rustle
fallen leaves,
rainsilt,
forgotten *night*bris

and I casually
turn,
too often,
   making sure
I walk alone

all the while
as if there is a
God
I am lit front and
back by advancing
and receding
lights
from shepherding
buses, taxis,
armies of cars
whose entire purpose
has been to shine
me home

We Are
by Elaine Starkman

we are not tintypes of
    great-grandmothers
who served men and bore sons
to sit at their feet in heaven

we are not portraits of
    grandmothers
who fled pogroms to make myths
in american sweatshops

we are not snapshots of
    mothers
doting in despair forcing us
into pink formals and mrs. degrees

we are a generation
seeking tradition
transforming symbols
    jewish women
not yet ourselves

First published in Coming Together, *Sheer Press, 1977.*

I Am Proud of You
by Chana Safran

I'm proud of you, sister of my time!
Proud of your tenacity, your advance
Your fought-for freedom.

On how many closed doors have you knocked
And with your will power and wisdom
Burst them open?
How many times have you kindled lights
And kept vigil over the ailing world?
Given healing and comfort
With your life-blood
For new generations
Created new values.

How often has your labor been ignored!
How often your achievements derided!
Yet, see!
Your deeds lift you up like stairs
You are climbing higher, higher
And your torch lights up the night.

Ancestor
by Frances Rodman

Susan was   the wild one
Who never would repent,
Looking through her finger,
Over prayerbook bent,
Heard a gypsy whistle
(Her eyes grew strangely still),
Came home again at midnight
Down a moon-washed hill.

They never spoke of Susan:
Her pictures were destroyed,
And what became of Susan
Was a subject to avoid.
But every late October
Her blood runs in my veins:
I hear her careless laughter
In silver autumn rains.

I put the thought of Susan
Behind me like a snare,
But there are dreams and wildness
That we together share.
And when I walk sedately
Across the village green,
I am the veriest hypocrite
The town has ever seen,

For part of me is running
Barefoot through the grass,
And most of me is drinking
October in a glass
Whose stain is rich and heady,
Whose taste is of the vine,
And from whose depths lost Susan
Stares back with eyes like mine. . . .

1950, United States.

The Limitations of Therapy
by Elizabeth Zelvin

Maria sits on the edge of her chair
waiting for the doctor to come.
The headset haloes her curly hair
her feet tap as if she were dancing
but she cannot hear the music.
The voices are too loud.

"Sit with me," says Maria,
"but don't you touch me!
The voices tell me I'm a bad girl
it's contagious, you know.
You'd be contaminated
one touch would set your blood on fire
it would send you up in flames.
I want to smash my fist through glass
and see the blood!"

Maria went four whole weeks without booze
because her daughter cried
but she needed smoke to make her sleep
and coke for loving.
Too much damaged loving
too many tongues, too many hands
too many voices.

"Help me!" cries Maria.
"I can't even hear the music.
They know the truth, my voices:
I'm a slut, a whore
I fuck for drugs.
They're shrieking for my blood
and I deserve it. Don't I?
Don't I?"

I want so much to touch her
to hold her hand
to hold her in my arms.
Leaning forward in my chair
I say, so gently, "You know,
you don't have to listen to those voices."
"That's just what they say about you!"
says Maria.

Susan Dances
by Beth Joselow

Maybe it was in all of her dancing,
Those kneebends practiced so steadily,
Those back-breaking arches
Pulled from a body that refused
To grow angles and kept to a
Motherly strength of curves —
A pigeon, all heart, all ribcage.

Maybe it was then
That she first learned what discipline
Can do. It can't make you a sure winner,
Or get you into the best dancing academy
In New York, but it can teach you
What to do with yourself after that

Because after that
Susan found God,
And trusted Him enough
To arrange her marriage;
She arched her back once more
And had a baby
And then two more.
She dances every Saturday night
At the synagogue, holding her
Handkerchief she swings,
She kicks, she points her toes
And knows that practicing
Is all there is.

B'Not Sarah
by Shulamith Surnamer

At the B'not Sarah Synagogue
the women
do it
all:

Ladies lead the T'filah,
        lain from the Torah,
                and learn a daf Gemora
    at services held
           each Rosh Chodesh day
  in a most creative
             and halachically correct way.

Hearing their sweet soprano supplications
        to HaElah HaGedolah,
            HaGiborah v'HaNorah

their prayers to HaSHEM
        MALKAT HaOLAM
            ELAT HaIMAHOT
        Sarah, Rivkah, Rachel v'Leah
    the SHEKHINAH feels renewed

and prepares for Her return
        Earthward
            from the highest Sephira.

Small Pleasures
by Nancy Imberman Tamler

Walking home from schul,
the January sun behind us,
we stand on California cobblestone, aligning our shadows,
forming a totem.
Waving on La Donna Ave., laughing.
This moment is fine and real.
Now I push the carriage and think
"A Mother in Israel."

My third decade filled; my third baby borne,
the shapely hourglass tells all and counts
my future; sands dripping moments.
Answers still in darkness, I see
a page of Talmud on the refrig,
beckoning for a glance during long kitchen hours.
My tikkun, given in love, for Chanukah, waiting patiently
on the shelf, counting the moons till Simhat Torah.

Leading the minyan, blessing
the overflowing cup of wine,
my quivering hand watches everyone assembled.
The children closely surrounding the laden table
sing
and wonder
along with me,
"Do women make kiddush in a room full of men?"
(We later fantasize hot-tub qua mikveh,
for both lovers,
renewing their cycle together.)

I am Rachel, struggling with Jacob's angel,
slowly climbing up ladders,
meeting real moments.
I weave my own coat of many colors
to wrap around me.
I will be as warm,
as rich,
as adorned
as the Earth, herself.

Women's Talk
by Helen Papell

Written after the first poetry reading at the Jewish Women's Resource Center.

The women go one by one aliyah
to the lectern to read a poem.
Skeleton in a recent mass grave, you are named
Daughter of Sarah.
Woman with womb locked as a tomb,
Chant these syllables to spin the moon's rays
and impel your egg in vitro.
Torah echoes these stanzas of women,

And yet, a child again under my father's tallit
in shul, I listen to scholars
step on Miriam's songs as though they are stones
on a man's path among the stars. I am told

Women are the ones who whisper
behind the mechitzah curtain, hidden
so their voices won't distract men.
The whispering always stops when I join them.
"What are they saying, Ma?"
"Women's talk."

The Sabbath morning my father decreed
I was now a girl, I left the shtetl
of his tallit. Behind the mechitzah, this day,
The women didn't stop talking.
Sarah also was an exile among her people, they said.
Miriam's song was recited by her brother Moses.

That afternoon, my mother let me brush
the red hair that fell like a hidden waterfall
to her waist. I watched the window for my father.
She pulled the phonograph to an inner wall,
Lifted skirt to her knees,
Danced a hora.

Miriam, my sister, come listen to your children
Skipping with your syllables
down the centuries of women.

First published in Up Against the Wall, Mother, *1986.*

Tsirl Waletzky

Glossary

accouchement. *French.* Confinement at childbirth.
Aktion. *German.* Military or police operation.
aleph. *Hebrew.* The first letter of the Hebrew alphabet; phonetically a "silent" letter.
aliyah. *Hebrew.* Going up. Used particularly for immigration to Israel: "going up to the land."
Amol iz geven. *Yiddish.* Once upon a time.
amot. *Hebrew.* Cubits. (A measure of distance.)
Ani Ma'amin. *Hebrew.* "I believe." The first words of the song, based on words of Maimonides, which Jewish martyrs sang on the way to their death: "I believe with perfect faith in the coming of the Messiah. Though he tarry, yet he will come."
Av. *Hebrew.* The month in the Hebrew calendar which approximates the month of August. Both the First Temple and the Second Temple were destroyed during this month.
bedecken. *Yiddish.* The ceremony just before a Jewish wedding, during which the groom covers the bride with the veil.
bet din. *Hebrew.* Court.
Beta Israel. *Hebrew.* Literally, House of Israel. The name which Ethiopian Jews apply to themselves.
b'not. *Hebrew.* Daughters of.
bobba. *Yiddish.* Grandmother.
bris, brit milah. *Hebrew.* The circumcision and naming through which a Jewish boy, usually on the eighth day of his life, enters the Covenant of Abraham with God.
brochah. *Hebrew.* Blessing.
challah. *Hebrew.* Specially shaped bread baked for Sabbath and

Holy Days; a piece of the dough has been taken out and ceremoniously burned before baking.

chametz. *Hebrew.* Leavened food, forbidden during the Festival of Passover.

Chanukah. *Hebrew.* Eight festive days commemorating the Jewish victory over the Seleucid Syrians and the rededication of the desecrated Temple.

Chava. *Hebrew.* Eve (proper name).

Chaye Sarah. *Hebrew.* "The life of Sarah." The opening phrase of the Torah portion which describes the death and burial of Sarah, the first Jewish matriarch.

Cheshbon Hanefesh. *Hebrew.* "Accounting of the soul"; self-examination of one's actions and motives.

chet. *Hebrew.* The eighth letter of the Hebrew alphabet.

daf Gemora. *Hebrew.* A page of Talmud.

das vedonya, tovarish. *Russian.* Good-bye, my friend.

dayeni. *Hebrew.* "Enough for me." A reference to "Dayenu"—"it would have been enough for us"—from the liturgy of the Seder, the first night of Passover.

Di kinder. *Yiddish.* The children.

dirham. *Arabic.* A coin.

dreidle. *Yiddish.* A special spinning top inscribed with Hebrew letters standing for the sentence "A great miracle happened there;" used for a game on Chanukah.

Ein Gedi. *Hebrew.* A spring and oasis in Judea, where David spent time while fleeing from Saul.

Elat HaImahot. *Hebrew.* Goddess of the matriarchs.

erev. *Hebrew.* Evening. Eve (of a Sabbath or Festival).

Eyt Ziknah. *Hebrew.* The time of old age. A reference to a prayer in the liturgy of the High Holy Days.

The Forward. A Yiddish newspaper published in New York.

frailach. *Yiddish.* Cheerful, festive.

Gaon. *Hebrew.* A great scholar.

G-d. Some pious Jews do not spell out the word "God."

goldeneh medineh. *Yiddish.* Golden country. Applied to the United States by Eastern European Jews in the late nineteenth and early twentieth century.

goyim. *Hebrew.* Nations. In Yiddish, applied to members of "other nations," Non-Jews.

ḥachamim. *Hebrew.* Sages.

ha Elah ha Gedolah. *Hebrew.* The great Goddess.

ḥag. *Hebrew.* Festival.

ha Giborah v'ha Norah. *Hebrew.* The Powerful One and Awesome One (feminine).

Haj. *Arabic.* Pilgrimage festival. In S. Ben-Tov's personal slang, the acronym for "hanging around Jerusalem."

halachah. *Hebrew.* The Jewish Law.

halachically. *Hebrew.* In accordance with Jewish Law.

Harey At. *Hebrew.* "Be thou." The opening words of the Jewish wedding formula. "Be thou consecrated to me . . ."

ha Shem. *Hebrew.* The Name. Used by pious Jews to refer to God.

Ḥasidim. *Hebrew.* Members of a movement in Orthodox Judaism which stresses prayer and joyful observance of the Law.

hechsher. *Hebrew.* Seal of approval placed by a rabbi upon ritually acceptable items, usually food items.

hondle. *Yiddish.* Making deals.

in vitro. *Latin.* Refers to the implantation in the uterus of an ovum fertilized in a laboratory.

Kabbalah. *Hebrew.* Literally, "tradition." Used of Jewish mysticism.

Kaddish. *Aramaic.* Prayer recited at public Jewish services, at intersections of parts of the liturgy. Specific recitals are by mourners.

Kaffeeklatch, koffee klatsch. *German.* Chat session over coffee.

kasher, kosher. *Hebrew.* Ritually fit to use, usually to eat.

kashered. *Yiddish.* Made ritually acceptable and pure.

knedalach. *Yiddish.* Round dumplings.

Kiddush. *Hebrew.* A blessing, usually over wine, recited on Sabbaths and Holy Days. Also, a collation offered with the Kiddush to a congregation in synagogue or home.

Kiddush Levana. *Hebrew.* Blessing of the new moon. Recited while standing out of doors on an evening between the 4th and 14th day of the lunar month when the moon is visible. Usually on a Saturday night; in the month of Av after Tishah b'Av, and in the month of Tishri after Yom Kippur.

Kohain. *Hebrew.* A priest, that is, a descendant of Aaron, brother of Moses. He is forbidden to "defile" himself by attending most funerals; it is his job to bless the congregation on sacred occasions.

Kol Nidre. *Aramaic.* "All vows . . ." A formula chanted before the sunset preceding Yom Kippur, releasing the congregation from forced vows.

Kri'ah. *Hebrew.* Tearing. At the graveside a tear is made in the clothing of the chief mourners, or in a ribbon symbolic of their clothing.

Kristallnacht. *German.* "Night of crystal." A mocking term used by Nazis to refer to the night of November 10, 1938, when they broke the windows and glassware of Jews.

Kvatterin. *Yiddish.* Godmother.

Lain. *Yiddish.* To read; usually applied to the reading of the Torah.

Lamed. *Hebrew.* The twelfth letter of the Hebrew alphabet.

licht. *Yiddish.* Light, lit candle. On the eve of Sabbaths and Holy Days, two or more candles are kindled.

ma mère. *French.* My Mother—applied to the Mother Superior of a convent.

Maabaroth. *Hebrew.* Temporary immigrant housing.

Malkat haOlam. *Hebrew.* Queen of the universe.

Mamushka. *Slavic Yiddish.* Grandmother.

Marrano. *Ladino.* A secret Jew, originally in 15th and 16th century Spain. Outwardly, the Marranos were practicing Catholics.

matzah. *Hebrew.* Large, flat unleavened crackers, eaten especially on Passover to commemorate the Biblical Exodus from Egypt.

Mazel tov. *Yiddish.* Good luck, congratulations.

medinah. *Arabic.* City center.

mechitzah. *Hebrew.* Partition between the men's and women's section in an Orthodox synagogue.

mezuzah. *Hebrew.* A parchment containing Biblical verses, attached in an ornamental case to the doorframes of Jewish homes.

midrash. *Hebrew.* Stories and moral teachings enhancing Biblical themes.

minyan. *Hebrew.* A quorum of ten eligible worshippers, required for a public prayer service.

mitzvah. *Hebrew.* An act prohibited or required by Jewish Law. Colloquially, a good deed.

Nachamu. *Hebrew.* "Comfort." The opening of the passage from Isaiah which is read on the Sabbath following the mourning fast of Tishah b'Av: "Comfort, comfort, my people, says the Lord."

nosh. *Yiddish.* Snack, nibble.

neksdorike. *Yiddish.* Next-door neighbor.

nuestro gente. *Spanish.* Our kinfolk.

nueva. *Spanish.* New (feminine).

Onkel. *German.* Uncle.

parve. *Yiddish.* Food that is neither meat nor dairy, hence may be served with either.

pasta al dente. *Italian.* Noodles cooked until just chewable, not too soft.

Pentacles. A suit in a pack of tarot cards.

Pesach. *Hebrew.* The Festival of Passover, which commemorates the Biblical Exodus from Egypt.

Purim. *Hebrew.* A merry, festive day commemorating the events in the Book of Esther.

Qiryat Shmoneh. *Hebrew.* An immigrant city in the Galilee, northern Israel.

rebbe. *Yiddish.* Teacher, rabbi.

Rebono. *Hebrew.* Master of the Universe.

Rosh Chodesh. *Hebrew.* "Head of the Month." The first day of every Hebrew month is celebrated as a minor festival.

Rozhinkes mit Mandlen. *Yiddish.* Raisins with almonds. Foods served on festive occasions to wish the company a sweet life.

Sabra. *Hebrew.* The fruit of the cactus plant, tough and prickly on the outside, sweet within—hence, a nickname for a native-born Israeli.

Sanhedrin. *Hebrew.* The ancient Jewish court of law.

schul, shul. *Yiddish.* Synagogue—a place of study and worship.

Sephira. *Hebrew.* Sphere.

Shabbat, Shabbes, Shabbos. *Hebrew.* Various transliterations of the Hebrew for Sabbath.

Shabes. *Yiddish.* Sabbath.

Shabes Licht. *Yiddish.* Sabbath candles, two or more, kindled before sunset on Friday evening to welcome the Sabbath, and promote tranquillity in the home.

Shekhinah. *Hebrew.* A grammatically feminine noun, referring to the indwelling presence of God in the world.

Shema. *Hebrew.* Hear! The opening word of the Jewish confession of faith, "Hear, Israel, the Lord our God the Lord is one."

Shevat. *Hebrew.* The month in the Jewish calendar when the trees begin to flower in Israel.

shtetl. *Yiddish.* A village or small town.

silentium mundi. *Latin.* The silence of the world.

simchah. *Hebrew, Yiddish.* Joyous occasion, celebration.

Simchat Torah. *Hebrew.* Rejoicing of the Law. The Festival which concludes the 22-day period of Holy Days in the autumn. On this day the reading of the Five Books of Moses is completed and begun again in the synagogue amid rejoicing and dance.

sin. *Hebrew.* The twenty-first letter of the Hebrew alphabet.

S'lach lanu, m'chal lanu, kaper lanu. *Hebrew.* "Forgive us, absolve us, grant us atonement"—an important prayer from the liturgy of Yom Kippur.

succah, suka, sukkah. *Hebrew.* A hut with a roof made of branches through which the stars can be seen, in which meals are enjoyed during the harvest Festival of Succoth commemorating the Jews' wanderings in the desert.

talis, talit. *Hebrew.* Prayer shawl.

Talmud. *Hebrew.* The primary body of Jewish Law.

Tante. *German.* Aunt.

te quiero. *Spanish.* I want you. I love you.

techinot. *Hebrew.* Prayers. Supplications. Usually in Yiddish, composed by and for women.

tefillin. *Hebrew.* Phylacteries. Leather boxes containing verses of Scripture which pious Jews wear, on their arm next to their heart and on their forehead, during weekday morning prayers.

Tels. A very small town in Eastern Europe which was a very great center of Jewish scholarship.

terra. *Latin.* Earth.

t'filah. *Hebrew.* Prayer.

tikkun. *Hebrew.* Rebuilding. Also, a certain type of prayer.

Tishah b'Av. *Hebrew.* The ninth day of the Hebrew month of Av, observed as a fast day to commemorate the destruction of the First Temple in the year 586 B.C.E. by the Babylonians and of the Second Temple by the Romans in 70 C.E.

Torah. *Hebrew.* Teaching. The Five Books of Moses. Also, the parchment scrolls, dressed in precious fabric, on which the Five Books of Moses are handwritten.

Tu b'Shvat. *Hebrew.* The fifteenth day of the Hebrew month of Shvat, celebrated as the New Year of the Trees.

Yahrzeit. *Yiddish.* Anniversary of a death. To commemorate the anniversary of the death of a close relative, a 24-hour candle is kindled in a glass.

yarmulke. *Yiddish.* Skull cap worn by pious Jews.

Yeshiva bocher. *Yiddish.* Student at a traditional rabbinical academy.

yizkor. *Hebrew.* Special prayer service in memory of the dead which is recited on Yom Kippur and on the three major Festivals.

yo soy marrano. *Spanish.* I am a Marrano.

Yom Kippur. *Hebrew.* Day of Atonement. A fast day, the most solemn day of the Jewish year, devoted to prayer, examination of one's actions, and renewal.

yosom. *Yiddish.* Orphan.

Index of First Lines

About once a week, inivited, I, 159
Abraham's eyes blaze the command to bathe his son, 13
All that long time, 148
All the vows, 194
Alone on Sunday, 125
And lo it came to pass, 216
And now—is the pain gone?, 180
and one week later, 173
And why, O King, my God, should the blood of a child, 12
Are we Jews sentenced to stay, 213
As our bodies took shape, 90
At night, 150
at 76 and 80 my parents buy new tennis rackets, 85
At six o'clock, my mother, 63
At the B'not Sarah Synagogue, 247
Bees celebrate Indian summer, 59
A Bialik tradition back home was, 193
Bible men walk, 228
big black man hugging the subway pole, 45
Birthing (then) and (now) parting, 161
Bitter is the word, 140
Come, come and listen, 157
convenient, my darling, 154
The courage to let go of the door, the handle, 32
Cultivated inside   out of the bounds, 187
Daughters of Sarah, 6
Death is not a striding reaper, 132
Death lives in our house, 174
Deep over me you bent your head, 2

Desire comes like the sea wind, 95
During the procedure, 233
each one had defenses, they said, 124
ever since I discovered, 2
The enemy is the dark, 125
Every Monday, the city herds, 164
the first swastika season, 70
The first time we made Shabbos together, 120
For the man who nurses, 47
Fresh is much better than frozen, 138
Friday morning, 30
The girls that are wanted are good girls, 232
"Go bang you head against the wall!", 30
Good evening Lord God, 212
Gray hairs, 172
Hallo, Reverend Mother? Hallo!, 188
Harry Saul wraps the leather strap of the tefillin box around his arm, 64
He came to say good-bye, 190
He lay on the hospital bed, 129
he talks so thick, 105
he'd stand out in the, 99
Here in the garden, 22
Holy grandmothers in Jerusalem, 230
Holy one of Being, 208
How I love to breathe the air of you, 33
I am sunned, 220
I cannot swim   but my parents, 184
I do not mind, 109
I dreamed that you appeared at my side, 74
I hate the Mundugumor, 143
I hated, 65

I have chopped the fish, 215
I have come back, 91
I have gone to the genealogy room, 106
I have searched, delved, studied, 223
I kissed the frog firmly . . . , 99
I know about the woman who sits and waits, 236
I know I don't look too good, 10
I know not your ways, 208
I needed a sin, 4
I never think of myself as waiting for you, 179
I packed all those important pieces, 49
I sleep, 151
I stood there shoulder to shoulder with the men, 145
I tried to live small, 128
I whisper "yo soy marrano", 104
I will leave my prison, 192
I will sit here very still, 18
If another flood should come, 184
If I squint I can see him in the field, that Jacob, 15
I'm beginning to forget names, faces, 169
I'm learning bones to please my father's ghost, 62
I'm of the tribe of Sarah, 202
I'm proud of you, sister of my time!, 243
In my head, 177
In the Medinah, in Marrakesh, 200
In the month of Av, 176
In Zerdova, 56
Isolate sepia people dying slowly, 202
It is April, 94
It is said that Abraham's tent, 7
It's to possess more than the skin, 112
I've seen Rachel tear at the strings, 17
Just outside the Ghetto wall, 191
A left eye that squints, 167
like a worried mother, 234

Long ago—one time, many times, 155
Mamushka, 34
Marcia Fogelson is dancing, 172
Maria sits on the edge of her chair, 245
Married academic woman ten, 84
Married to one man, 18
Maybe it was in all of her dancing, 246
Midwinter yet it has started, 219
Millennia have swept across the sands, 231
Mother's annoying everyone again, 168
Mrs. Lane lives alone now, 175
My brother and I were at Sinai, 224
My brother's father-in-law kept boiled wine, 40
My father balances on scaffolding, 69
My father belonged, 66
My father was the silence that we ate, 55
My father would sing to me, 55
My four sisters, 197
My grandfather Pesach hung himself, 46
My Jewish life scribbled, 131
My old neighbor isn't in the apartment any more, 38
My psychiatrist, having turned eighty, 165
nipple-length, 113
Nowadays they wear, 145
Nowadays your father couldn't play his trick, 14
O my God! Soon, soon approaches the great hour, 140
Of course the restaurant was open, 196
on the second anniversary of Liberation, 255
On the tenth of November, 72
Once I was at a wedding, 112
Once upon a time in Concord, California, there lived a woman of valor with, 126

the other women watching, 240
the pale eyes flashing in his dark face, 101
Pale moon, 206
Patience is the lesson, 97
Peace, the hour, 54
Pigeons see me as a five foot five, 138
The place was Poland Warsaw, 188
The pot itself was half the story, 68
Rebono, 156
Remember the hill where we played, 16
Round bellied sisters, 51
Sclerotic means the scars are all inside, 171
Shall I put on this Kri'ah?, 180
She had thought the studio would keep itself, 108
She said you'll find what you need here, 141
She tosses bread to them, 43
Sitting in the park, 168
a sparrow hops in the lilac on the arab side of our house, 218
Speak to me. Take my hand. What are you now?, 97
The subway beggar crouches against the token booth, 44
Sunday nights at 7, he's here, 29
The sunflowers are turning, 220
Susan was the wild one, 244
That happy multiplying, 235
There I was and I was parve, 238
There is a black thread, 199
These days of love are lollipops, 119
they did not build wings for them, 41
the thing about you and me: 88

This is the end of Brooklyn, defiant and salty, 76
Though years divide, we're sisters yet, 23
A thousand lamps for you in the curve of the shore, 198
Today it matters, that I hold, 31
Too long have I mourned the passing of many springs, 178
Toward evening, the sun has fired, 227
Two days a week I teach. I try, 107
Under a sky the color of pea soup, 226
Walking home from schul, 248
We are not tintypes of great-grandmothers, 242
We were bridesmaids in the same wedding, 118
What can be wrong, 122
What does it matter, 222
When Risa crosses her long legs, 239
When young women leave home, 88
Where are we? my Ishmael sings, 8
Whose smile is that?, 117
Why do you say my sound is "ah"?, 116
The women go one by one, aliyah, 249
The women, hair wrapped in colorful scarves, 203
Yeshiva handsome, 102
You grasp your cane with the hunger, 166
You sowed in me, not a child, 121
You were luckier than I, 13
Your arrival was always with cashews, 26

Index of Last Lines

about to join you, 13
across the field, the water pipes are singing, 227
after the long season of tending and growth, the harvest comes, 226
all over the back of my mind, 145
among the grasses of the field, 54
and all the beautiful marble columns broken, 109
and catches his breath, 94
And down to deeper roots to be reborn, 232
and falling back, 49
and gave it to the cold November morning, 235
and how the nights are cold, 124
and I am bitter in my doubts, 12
And indeed we have bloomed through the years, 120
And knows that practicing is all there is, 246
and my eyes elsewhere, 45
and one always said, be serious, 222
and raise pigs, 104
And screw the caterer, 112
And smite the sea with thunder for its sins, 184
And the rest of the town, 196
And the whole universe will sing, 74
And those who pick them up, 38
And we try to get them to look, 6
and what that meant, 31
And you dreaming the same, 128
And your torch lights up the night, 243
anything differently, 106
The aroma of Sabbath-candles and naphthalene, 230

as adorned as the Earth, herself, 248
because I felt so lonely with you, 125
blue blossoms hang low on the bush, 215
bobbing unpedestalled, 105
bring them to you, 91
brushing and combing us, 26
-But my life and line continue-, 131
cleansing orange against wheat, 200
curled on our sides like harbors, 95
a daughter pulling an enemy child from this river?, 202
devouring what is already lost, 203
Do others feel like this? Where do they go?, 122
down the centuries of women, 249
each not knowing the language of the other, 46
Either she's grown up. Or I, 159
the empty holes grown shut, 193
Even today, he'll have her too, 14
everywhere but here, 8
exercising power, 15
Fiercely resisting princehood, 99
a final act of love, 63
for my companion vowel, 116
for the glory of the heaven beyond the stars, 178
for us both, 16
forgotten dreams, 155
from cold-cuts. And stale bread, 43
from the highest Sephira, 247
four amot away from death, 176
Garlands alone in the night, 22
gathers shadows, 168
Give them comfort in the night, 212
God is deaf, 165
Goodbye, dear friend, 34

has been to shine me home, 240
Have been grafted onto mine, 197
have my duty to perform, 84
having so much to lose, 85
he gave me cool water in a yahrzeit glass, 125
He puts the veil down over her face, 117
he/she does spin, 113
Help us feel Your presence always, 208
his silence the rock inside the stone, 55
his sometimes pissass ways, 99
I am afraid of the dark, 208
I give birth to you   little tree, 141
I have the right, 138
I never touched them, 70
I still, even now, can make you songs, 121
I wait for you to come, 97
I wake up, 56
"I wish that I could wear one," 188
if anything will ever come of it, 234
if the world survives, 88
In my husband's name, 4
in the rush of spring, 239
in winter, 175
in your eyes, 90
it didn't matter, 225
It was almost dark, 184
jewish women not yet ourselves, 242
Keep and preserve me from all evil. Amen, 140
a late bloomer—but special, 18
the layers of our lives, 29
leaving a thin scar?, 161
let them tango, 166
like a relentless milkman up the stairs, 108
A man of valor, who can find?, 126
marrying   marrying, 118
matzas made out of oats?, 156
May you be comforted, 180
mothers taught them, 88
music to my ears!, 30

my children not be taken for my sins, 40
My Mirele, so long till then, 188
my missed-child missing, 140
my mother my father?, 177
my own set of dishes, 238
my wind-up doll, 65
No entry papers needed anymore, 190
not yet   not yet, 173
not yet visible, 69
I now dare to leave the darkness of this place, 192
Now it's you, 148
Now let my day begin!, 132
of a public shelter, 44
of home-grown Ḥachamim, 213
of the ward, 172
the oldest sound I know, 169
on any rock, 138
on whose tree it grew?, 157
One, 33
One moon inside both of us now, 51
or receive the light, 220
Or startle at the shadows that lengthen by my side, 107
Our children eat, grow beautiful on the mountain, 198
Our lives consist of what we choose to hide, 171
Outside the music plays, 191
Perhaps even to love them, 194
Rejoice!, 206
Said Leah, 18
Saved by Mommy, 72
she makes the man oatmeal and coffee, 64
she might follow, 13
shows buds beginning blossoms, 219
So warmly, warmly good. Amen, 216
"So when can I do it again?", 167
sparks flying, 224
Speak to me, 97
Stares back with eyes like mine, 244
sticks in his throat, 2
still holding in the sun, 76

Straightened his hat, 102
strangers as you are even to your own kin?, 202
taste it, 30
that I am beginning to open the book, 180
"That's just what they said about you!" says Maria, 245
their plates with more, 199
there are also the motionless Junipers, 218
There's constant and steady demand, 232
they do not know I loved you, 101
the things aesthetical," 68
things will not stop blooming, 47
to anyone's dart, 172
to begin, 151
to come back on, 59
to put your arms around me, 154
To the Braille of the underside, 55
together with the bitter flavor of the last, 164
too long without flowers, with broken wings, 220
touched her face, 17
The tunnel was sealed at both ends from the start, 10
turn down the sheet, 174

walking silently in the paths of her ancestors, 7
The water of the lake rests nearby sparkling, 223
We make amends in any way we can, 62
What do you need with all those foreskins anyway?, 145
When I am better, 233
where he belonged the most, 66
Who also love whom I despise, 23
who became other by saving themselves, 32
who hopes for her daughter not to sit and wait, 236
why you've left me here alone, 179
will anyone notice when I disintegrate?, 160
will shift the balance of the universe, 112
wind-stunned, 119
with one golden spoon, 223
With savage hues of our captivity, 187
would visit it at night baring her breasts to the moon, 41
You bent your head deep over me-, 2
You won't be sorry, 150
your serious face, 143
-You're with me, I replied, 129